HOW (NOT) TO BE A Tyrant

How (Not) to Be a Tyrant

Ten Lessons on Life and Leadership from the Bible's Worst Rulers

JOSHUA W. JIPP

BrazosPress
a division of Baker Publishing Group
Grand Rapids, Michigan

Published by Brazos Press
a division of Baker Publishing Group
Grand Rapids, Michigan
BrazosPress.com

Printed in the United States of America

Library of Congress Cataloging-in-Publication Data
Names: Jipp, Joshua W. author
Title: How (not) to be a tyrant : ten lessons on life and leadership from the Bible's worst rulers / Joshua W. Jipp.
Description: Grand Rapids, Michigan : Brazos Press, a division of Baker Publishing Group, [2026]
Identifiers: LCCN 2026013598 | ISBN 9781587437205 paperback | ISBN 9781493477807 ebook
Subjects: LCSH: Leadership—Biblical teaching | Christian life—Biblical teaching | Bible—Criticism, interpretation, etc.
Classification: LCC BS680.L4 J57 2026
LC record available at https://lccn.loc.gov/2026013598

Any italics used in Scripture quotations has been added for emphasis.

Cover design by Darren Welch Design
Interior design by William Overbeeke

Baker Publishing Group publications use paper produced from sustainable forestry practices and postconsumer waste whenever possible.

26 27 28 29 30 31 32   7 6 5 4 3 2 1

CONTENTS

PROLOGUE
The Way of Jesus vs. the Way of Satan

Give the king your justice, O God, and your righteousness to a king's son. May he judge your people with righteousness, and your poor with justice. May the mountains yield prosperity for the people, and the hills, in righteousness. May he defend the cause of the poor of the people, give deliverance to the needy, and crush the oppressor. . . . He delivers the needy when they call, the poor and those who have no helper. He has pity on the weak and the needy, and saves the lives of the needy.

—Psalm 72:1–4, 12–13

He has brought down the powerful from their thrones, and lifted up the lowly.

—Luke 1:52

What type of leader do you admire? Give it some thought. The leader could be a pastor, a politician, a coach, the head of an organization or business, a teacher, or anyone else entrusted with a measure of power and influence based on their role. What is it that you admire and respect? More directly, I want to know if you admire the person's character—their wisdom, humility, and service, perhaps—or if you are more impressed by their reputation for getting results, having irresistible charisma, drawing numbers, and influencing people.

It's Hard to Argue with the Results!

We have all seen how powerful people in all types of organizations have a way of validating their leadership by emphasizing their results, effectiveness, and achievements. How often have you heard some version of the following?

> "Well, they get the job done."
> "But it's hard to argue with the results!"
> "I love a leader who calls it like they see it!"

Or maybe a leader's transgressions are overlooked because the church or organization is experiencing increased profits, positive media visibility, or growing numbers of members and followers. These are often interpreted as signs of the leader's effectiveness, perhaps even indicating God's favor and blessing on the leader.

Think of the following fictional (but easy to relate to) examples of leaders in both secular and Christian settings:

> The revered basketball coach, seemingly admired by the entire state, whose verbal and even physical abuse of his players (and, on occasion, of even referees and fans) is mostly winked at, given the conference and national titles that hang from the arena's rafters.

> The seminary president who runs the school with a culture of fear and intimidation, surrounding himself with deans, advisers, and board members who enable him to "protect the gospel" and save theological orthodoxy from the liberals—albeit at the expense of any who disagree, question his leadership style, or ask difficult questions.

> The megachurch pastor, a gifted and passionate giver of sermons, who planted his church and has now expanded it into a multistate conglomerate of churches with a massive media presence but who solidifies his position through manipulation and bullying, whose anger and

verbal abuse terrifies all dissenters, and who refuses to admit wrongdoing or a need to seek forgiveness.

The pragmatic politician who uses any and every means available, including manipulation, coercion, fearmongering, and bullying, in order to implement his policies and to solidify his grip on his office and punish his enemies.

All of these examples embody aspects of tyrannical leadership that are exposed by the Christian Scriptures as antithetical to the way of life and leadership that Jesus calls his followers to adopt. But the prevalence of this "tyrant option" among leaders, and its validation by the supposed results it procures, has led too many followers of Jesus to adopt a non-Christian approach to leadership that prioritizes results and effectiveness over Jesus-like character.

Maybe you're not a basketball coach, seminary president, megachurch pastor, or politician. But you almost certainly have spaces where you exert influence and power through your decision-making and have people who look up to you, depend on you, and trust you as an example of how to live in the world. The Bible's stories of bad leaders, kings, and rulers are there to remind us that followers of Jesus must reject the way of the tyrant. My hope is that by looking at the stories of the Bible's worst rulers and then contrasting them with the positive example offered in the life and teachings of Jesus—as well as through important stories and laws in the Old Testament—you will be able to steward your influence in a way that testifies to the goodness and beauty of the way of King Jesus.

SATAN-INSPIRED LEADERSHIP

Two forms of leadership, two radically different ways of using power and authority, are presented in the initial encounter between Jesus and Satan in the wilderness (Matt. 4:1–11; Mark 1:12–13; Luke 4:1–13). When Jesus rejects Satan's temptation to use his power for fame, food and drink, and personal glory, he shows us that his life will embody a rejection of a use of power that would ultimately transform him into an exploitative, abusive tyrant. Instead, Jesus's kingship testifies to a different type of power, one that is revealed in love, service, humility, and truth-telling. Jesus's kingly use of power—to rescue and save a people through giving his life for them—stands against the constant temptation to use power for personal benefit even if it means using oppression and coercion against others.

Jesus succeeded in resisting the temptation of Satan, but Satan's temptation of Jesus's followers is still an ever-present reality. In fact, one of the main tasks of Satan throughout the Scriptures is to deceive God's people, to tempt them to turn away from God in their daily lives and choices. All too frequently, Christians are deceived by Satan into thinking that they can use aspects of the tyrant option in order to achieve Christian goals. But Jesus shows us that the tyrant option for leadership is nothing new, and that it is a way of leadership and life that followers of Jesus must reject.

Will Jesus's people follow his way and embrace a life marked by love of our enemies, forgiveness of those who wrong us, and speaking the truth even at great personal cost?

The argument of this book is that prioritizing effectiveness and results in Christian leadership at the expense of Christian character is the way of Satan. And this form of Satan-inspired leadership is prevalent in many of our Christian churches, schools, and organizations.

Positing results and effectiveness as a leader's ultimate good to be pursued at all costs will invariably draw the leader into a situation where it's impossible to follow Jesus's call for truth-telling, service, hospitality to strangers, mercy and care for the most vulnerable, forgiveness, and other essential aspects of Christian character. The way of Jesus is compromised when it is not seen as the best method for getting results. And Satan's work is to deceive us into thinking that our endowment, our reputation, our influence in the media, our enrollment, or the number of people in our churches is the ultimate mark of Christian success.

The argument of this book is certainly not that Christian leaders should be incompetent or disinterested in appropriately wielding their influence and in obtaining results. An argument of this nature would be patently absurd. This book is instead a call for leaders and followers alike to live their lives and exert their influence in a way that is consistent with King Jesus, not the tyrants that populate the landscape of Scripture.

Why Are There So Many Stories of Bad Rulers in the Bible?

The storyline of the Christian Bible does not make sense apart from its narrative of wicked tyrants and evil rulers who oppress God's people, who are culpable for putting John the Baptist and Jesus to death, and who, sadly, even come from within God's people to exploit them. These tyrannical rulers are not incidental to the message of the Bible. They provide a constant reminder to God's people that they must reject the ways of Pharaoh, that Christ's use of power is directly antithetical to that of Herod and Pilate, and that central to God's plan is his promise to provide a peace-loving, mercy-bestowing, hospitable king to lead his people in a new way of life. These tyrants offer a constant reminder to God's people that any attempt to establish God's purposes through violence, deception, or coercion is ultimately the path of Satan.

The Bible, therefore, has an ambivalent but realistic take on the institution of kingship. On the one hand, the beautiful prayer for the king in Psalm 72, among numerous other biblical texts, testifies to God's plan to rule the world through a good king who loves justice and righteousness, leads the people in prosperity, provides generously, and brings justice for the poor and the vulnerable. Israel's prophets have amazing expectations that a king will come from the house of David who will embody wisdom and righteousness, love God completely and entirely, and usher in a reign of peace (Isa. 11:1–5; Jer. 23:1–5)—a shepherd-king who will tend his flock with gentleness, will feed and nourish them, and will not exploit or harm the weak and vulnerable but compassionately care for them (Ezek. 34:11–31). These prophetic expectations take as their starting point God's unbreakable covenant and promise made to King David that one of his sons will have a kingdom and a reign that will last forever (2 Sam. 7:12–14). And, of course, the New Testament portrays Jesus the Messiah as the promised king who generously provides justice and peace for all who take refuge in him.

On the other hand, many of the atrocities narrated in the Bible are the result of wicked tyrants. The laws in the Torah set forth a way of life for God's people that is directly antithetical to their experience of the tyrannical regime of Pharaoh in Egypt. Rather than exploiting the immigrant as Pharaoh did, God's people are to welcome the stranger and provide justice and equity for the stranger living in their land. Instead of operating within a Pharaoh-like extractive and greedy economy, God's people are called to cancel debts and share what God has given them. The Gospels also carry on an ongoing comparison between Jesus's kingship and the flawed, oppressive, and violent rule enacted by human rulers. As we will see, Herod, Pilate, and others entrusted with imperial authority and rule are exposed as fraudulent counterfeits of the good king. Jesus's messianic kingship of truth and justice exposes the pretense of the unjust and the corrupt rule of tyrants, thereby calling the Messiah's people to embody practices oriented toward peace, justice, and generosity.

We will see that the Bible's frequent depiction of tyrants who use deceit, manipulation, and brute force to accomplish their agendas provides a consistent reminder of the nature of Christ's kingship and his surprising use of power for good.

In what follows, we will look at ten lessons Christian leaders can learn to help them avoid using their power like tyrants. This book provides ten key characteristics, strategies, and tactics of bad rulers that can be used as a lens for evaluating how leaders, and we ourselves, use power and influence. These lessons have implications for all followers of Jesus, because the ten leadership principles of these tyrants function as a foil to Christ's kingship and to the way of discipleship that his followers are called to. We will see that tyrants use power in an abusive and oppressive manner to benefit themselves and the few elites who surround them. Tyrants use power for personal gain rather than serving the good and flourishing of one's people. And this is the absolute antithesis to Christ's kingship and his kingdom.

REFLECTION QUESTIONS

1. Do you have any personal experiences or stories that come to mind of a leader whose success and effectiveness (in worldly standards) allowed them to get away with improper, even ungodly, decisions and character traits?
2. Why do you think the Bible includes so many stories of bad rulers but comparatively fewer stories of good ones? Is this a historical accident or is it an indication of something more significant about power and the world we live in?

1

Extract, Exploit, and Enslave

Pharaoh

The Egyptians became ruthless in imposing tasks on the Israelites, and made their lives bitter with hard service in mortar and brick and in every kind of field labor. They were ruthless in all the tasks that they imposed on them.

—Exodus 1:13–14

The term "Pharaoh" was, at least initially, not a proper name but a title that designated the Egyptian royal palace. Identifying the specific rulers referred to in Genesis and Exodus by the title of Pharaoh is difficult, perhaps impossible. What is most important to note is that Pharaoh plays the theological and literary role of God's enemy. Pharaoh's economic policies play a decisive role in the rest of the Old Testament, as they embody a way of life marked by economic exploitation that God consistently calls his people to reject. God's humiliation of Pharaoh provides a reminder to all who read of his demise that God stands against the tyrannical use of power to exploit others.

Good economic policies exist, or are supposed to exist, to serve the flourishing of an entire society. The good life for a collective people requires the careful ordering of civilization so that people are capable of working, farming, building, and cultivating to provide what is needed for themselves and those who depend on their work.

Tyrants and empires are committed instead to a form of ordering wealth, production, and material goods that has little, if any, basis in a vision of economics as contributing to the good life of the entire populace. Extraction (the forced removal of wealth by the powerful), acquisition, and personal greed are the motivating principles used to contribute to the good of the king and the elites, rather than to the good of individuals, households, and society. Pharaoh embodies a way of life that is devoted to using land, livestock, and labor for himself and his royal palace rather than for his people.

Running throughout the first five books of the Bible is God's promise to give his people a home, a place where they can live in peaceful harmony with God, the land, and one another (Gen. 12:1–4; 15:16–21). In fact, the lengthy blocks of commandments and regulations in the Torah are given to instruct God's people in how they might have a harmonious and flourishing relationship with God and with their fellow humans when they enter into their land. But standing in the way of the fulfillment of this promise is the exploitative and extractive regime of Egypt and Pharaoh.

PHARAOH'S ECONOMY

Lest one think that Pharaoh's economic policy would take advantage of foreigners *only*, Genesis depicts Pharaoh as exploiting his own people by taking all of the land of Egypt for himself during a period of great crisis. We see here a fundamental principle of tyrants: Use periods of upheaval to declare a state of emergency, whereby one has free rein to enact self-serving policies and personal agendas. So when a severe famine comes on Egypt, the people beg Joseph: "There is nothing left in the sight of my lord but our bodies and our lands. . . . Buy us and our land in exchange for food. We with our land will become slaves to Pharaoh" (Gen. 47:18–19). All the Egyptians give up their property such that "the land became Pharaoh's" (v. 20). This is a common tactic among tyrannical rulers and one that will mark the history of the Egyptians for centuries to come—namely, a centralized economy centered on a king who owns and controls the land.

The Egyptian farmers thus become slaves who work Pharaoh's land: "[Joseph] made slaves of them from one end of Egypt to the other" (47:21). The Egyptians are required to give 20 percent of their harvest to Egypt every year. While this is perhaps an effective strategy in a time of crisis, Pharaoh uses the crisis as an opportunity to establish his ownership of the land through a high taxation rate as a *permanent statute* (v. 26). Whereas the Torah mandates that it is God who is the owner of the land (Lev. 25:23), Pharaoh does not release the land back to the people but keeps it permanently under his possession and ownership.

It is no great surprise that, later, Joseph's family and their descendants find themselves under the exploitative rule of another Egyptian Pharaoh whose acquisitiveness and excessive greed leads him to enslave the Israelites so that they can build supply cities (Exod. 1:8–14). The narrator underscores the brutality of the work imposed on the Israelites:

> "Therefore [the Egyptians] set taskmasters over [the Israelites] to *oppress them with forced labor.*" (Exod. 1:11)
>
> "But the more they were *oppressed*, the more they multiplied." (1:12)
>
> "The Egyptians became *ruthless* in imposing tasks on the Israelites." (1:13)
>
> They "made their *lives bitter with hard service*. . . . They were *ruthless* in all the tasks that they imposed on them." (1:14)

Israel suffers under this situation for a long time, but God's way is not the way of Pharaoh! Instead, God has compassion on his oppressed people: "The Israelites groaned under their slavery, and cried out. Out of the slavery their cry for help rose up to God. God heard their groaning, and God remembered his covenant with Abraham, Isaac, and Jacob" (Exod. 2:23–24). God's redemption of his people in the exodus story, then, is an explicit act of judgment on Pharaoh's economic regime marked by greed and exploitation of human life.

Pharaoh's regime and Israel's experience of slavery in Egypt is sadly not the last of its kind in Israel's history. Other foreign empires will impose heavy, even impossible, taxes and tributes on God's people, such as in the book of Nehemiah, which was written during the Persian rule of Judah (558–331 BCE). Nehemiah depicts a situation where Persian overseers collaborate with elite members of the Judean ruling class to collect taxes from ordinary laborers and farmers. Persia's extractive economic policies are described in Nehemiah 5:1–5, a text that echoes the policies of Pharaoh:

> There was a great outcry of the people and of their wives against their Jewish kin. For there were those who said, "With our sons and our daughters, we are many; we must get grain, so that we may eat and stay alive." There were also those who said, "We are having to pledge our fields, our vineyards, and our houses in order to get grain during the famine." And there were those who said, "We are having to borrow money on our fields and vineyards to pay the king's tax. Now our flesh is the same as that of our kindred; our children are the same as their children; and yet we are forcing our sons and daughters to be slaves, and some of our daughters have been ravished; we are powerless, and our fields and vineyards now belong to others."

Again, we find that the powerful are willing to use crisis as an opportunity to exploit the economically vulnerable, creating a situation of debt bondage that causes Israel to "cry out" for justice, just as it did in the time of the exodus (Exod. 2:23–25). Nehemiah demands that the wealthy nobles stop this practice of excessive extraction, and he discontinues the wicked policies of earlier Jewish governors who had profited off their own kin through predatory economic policies (Neh. 5:6–15).

HOW NOT TO BE A TYRANT: Generous Economics

Instead of furthering an economy marked by extraction, exploitation, and enslavement, disciples of King Jesus are called to live generously, using their wealth, resources, and material goods so that all can flourish.

GENEROUS ECONOMICS

God's redemption of Israel from Pharaoh reveals God's opposition to all forms of economic systems imposed by the powerful that would destroy human life. And in gifting land to Israel, God envisions Israel flourishing and living together in justice and peace. God's opposition to Pharaoh's extractive, exploitative economic regime is intended to be reflected in Israel's economic practices as set forth in the Torah.

First, God's people are called to reject greed and wealth accumulation at the expense of their neighbors. This is most evident in the prohibition against covetousness: "You shall not covet your neighbor's house; you shall not covet your neighbor's wife, or male or female slave, ox, or donkey, or anything that belongs to your neighbor" (Exod. 20:17). The book of Deuteronomy exemplifies the dangers of forgetting God as the divine gift-giver and of turning toward greed and acquisition. Moses warns, for example, that Israel must be careful lest they forget God once they enter into the land and experience the material goods of cisterns, vineyards, and olive groves (Deut. 6:10–15). He warns again two chapters later,

> When you have eaten your fill and have built fine houses and live in them, and when your herds and flocks have multiplied, and your silver and gold is multiplied, and all that you have is multiplied, then do not exalt yourself, forgetting the Lord your God, who brought you out of the land of Egypt, out of the place of slavery. (Deut. 8:12–14)

Once Israel forgets God as the divine gift-giver, their sense of economic self-sufficiency invariably leads to the same greedy economic exploitation of others as Pharaoh's.

Second, whereas the tyrant option allows Pharaoh to own the land, God's ownership of the land means that God's people must engage in periodic debt cancellations. God declares: "The land shall not be sold in perpetuity, for the land is mine; with me you are but aliens and tenants" (Lev. 25:23). For this reason, there is to be a seven-year cycle where debts are canceled and a fifty-year period where land is restored to those who have fallen on difficult times (Lev. 25:8–17, 24–28). Further, if an Israelite cannot provide for himself or make good on a loan, his fellow Israelite is commanded to take care of him and to not charge him any interest on the loan (vv. 35–37, 39–46). Why? The theological foundation is clear: "I am the LORD your God, who brought you out of the land of Egypt, to give you the land of Canaan, to be your God" (v. 38).

Similar commands to forgive people their economic debts are the focus of Deuteronomy 15. The first verse sets the focus: "Every seventh year you shall grant a remission of debts" (Deut. 15:1). Moses commands Israel not to be "hard-hearted or tight-fisted toward your needy neighbor" but to "open your hand, willingly lending enough to meet the need, whatever it may be" (vv. 7–8). Remarkably, the goal of Israel's obedience to God's economy is that there will "be no one in need among you" (v. 4).

Third, Moses writes that financial dealings must not be guided by profiteering from the poverty of a fellow neighbor. For example, moneylenders are not to act like moneylenders when giving loans, not charging interest to the poor person (Exod. 22:25). Further, if they take a neighbor's clothing as collateral, the creditor must give it back to the debtor before sunset (vv. 26–27). One wonders whether this is simply a veiled way of telling the creditor not to take collateral from a poor person. The Israelites must realize that economic transactions *always* involve the third party, Yahweh. Hence, the creditor should be warned that if the poor person is exploited and he cries out to God—as the Israelites did when they were oppressed by Pharaoh—then God may respond with judgment against those who oppress the poor, for God says, "I will listen, for I am compassionate" (v. 27).

Jesus was born into a situation where the vast majority of Israelites were oppressed both by wealthy landowners within ancient Palestine and by taxes and tributes imposed by Rome. The result was that most people were burdened by increasing indebtedness, and many were displaced as tenant workers, day laborers, and peasant farmers who hoped to make just enough to provide for their family.

Jesus's preaching thus calls for economic release and freedom for those oppressed by Pharaoh-style economics. In fact, Jesus's public sermon in the Gospel of Luke echoes the biblical texts about Jubilee that we've already examined:

> The Spirit of the Lord is upon me, because he has anointed me to bring good news to the poor. He has sent me to proclaim release to the captives and recovery of sight to the blind, to let the oppressed go free, to proclaim the year of the Lord's favor. (Luke 4:18–19)

The language of "release" and "go free" echoes God's institution of the practice of Jubilee in Leviticus 25, where debts are to be canceled, the enslaved are to go free, and fellow Israelites are reminded that it is God who owns the land. Jesus testifies to a radically different way of economics than what we see exemplified by tyrants. The earliest Christians practiced Jesus's economics in a variety of ways, such as

- giving to the poor (Luke 11:41; Gal. 2:10),
- selling one's property for the common good (Acts 4:36–37),
- contributing to people's needs in times of famine (2 Cor. 8–9)

- advocating for just and fair wages for day laborers (James 5:1–6),
- rejecting greed and excessive consumption (Luke 12:13–21; 16:13–15),
- generously providing support for missionaries or widows (Phil. 4:10–20; 1 Tim. 5:3–16),
- giving gifts and loans to those who can't repay (Luke 14:7–14)

Similarly, there are a variety of ways that disciples of King Jesus can practice his economic teachings today. Jesus's disciples recognize that just as God's ownership of the land was the starting point for Israel's economic practices, so also everything we have is a good gift from God (Luke 6:35; 12:24–28; James 1:17). Our lives do not wholly consist of what we have or consume, and so we commit to both advocating for and generously sharing God's gifts with those in need.

You have likely heard numerous examples of Christians who have practiced Jesus's economy in publicly heroic as well as quietly faithful ways. I think of those who have founded hospitals or have used their financial resources to alleviate suffering in places that lacked basic medical care. Some Christians have rescued children from infanticide or cared for orphans. Some have faithfully given of their time and wealth to care for the financially vulnerable or have hosted fundraisers for those going through emergencies. Others have fought for fair and just wages for day laborers, minorities, and immigrants. These examples and many more provide a powerful and consistent witness against a way of life, often seen in leaders, marked by greed and exploitation of the vulnerable.

REFLECTION QUESTIONS

1. Can you think of any examples of institutions or businesses that accrue wealth by exploiting the most vulnerable in our society? What, if anything, should followers of Jesus do in response?
2. What are some specific challenges leaders face in practicing generous economics?

2

Stoke Fear of Others

Pharaoh

Now a new king arose over Egypt, who did not know Joseph. He said to his people, "Look, the Israelite people are more numerous and more powerful than we. Come, let us deal shrewdly with them, or they will increase and, in the event of war, join our enemies and fight against us and escape from the land."

—Exodus 1:8–10

Pharaoh played the central role in Egyptian society, religion, and politics. He was judge, lawgiver, head priest, and perhaps considered semidivine. Pharaoh's divine kingship also meant that his job was to ensure the fertility of the land and to maintain proper and peaceful order between his human subjects and the gods. Pharaoh in the book of Exodus exhibits the common approach of using fearmongering to exploit immigrants who reside in the land. These Hebrews, he says, threaten Egypt's national security and therefore should be treated as an invasive species who deserve to be exploited and treated violently.

When the leader of a nation faces serious challenges, whether it be to economics, social cohesion, or the rule of law, an all-too-common tactic is to demonize the immigrants and foreigners who live in that nation. Immigrants, so the rhetoric goes, do not contribute to the economy, are leaches on the health care system, are violent criminals, take away the jobs of citizens, threaten national security, and pollute a stable cultural identity and history. They are not spoken of as humans but as "illegals," "criminals," and "invaders." They are dehumanized and considered garbage from worthless countries, people who poison society by their mere presence. It doesn't matter if these claims are even believable or backed by evidence; what matters is that the anti-immigrant rhetoric effectively directs attention away from any blame the ruler might receive and instead stokes fear about how foreigners are harming and contaminating. This works to create a strong contrast between "us" and "them." And it allows the tyrant to use foreigners for economic profit. We see Pharaoh in the book of Exodus doing exactly this, embodying a way of life that is directly antithetical to God's vision for a good people and society.

PHARAOH'S INHOSPITALITY

After Jacob and his family discover that Joseph is still alive and then reconcile with him, Jacob's family seeks to immigrate to Egypt due to a severe famine (Gen. 46:8–34). The brothers appeal to Pharaoh: "We have come to reside as aliens in the land; for there is no pasture for your servants' flocks because the famine is severe in the land of Canaan" (47:4). Pharaoh extends hospitality to Jacob and the brothers by allowing the family to come and resettle "in the best part of the land" (47:6, 11).

The book of Exodus begins with a reminder that Jacob and his sons and their families have resettled in Egypt due to the famine (Exod. 1:1–6). But when a new Pharaoh, who has no knowledge of Joseph, comes into power, he reverses the policy of the previous Pharaoh and engages in fearmongering tactics to reduce Jacob's family to slaves. He claims that the Israelite people are too large and powerful and that they have the potential to turn into enemies of Egypt who may fight against them and threaten their way of life. The new Pharaoh uses this fearmongering to subject the vulnerable immigrant Israelites to harsh labor. Exodus repeatedly uses the words "ruthless" and "bitter" to describe the work imposed on Israel (1:13–14). Despite the Israelite people having recently benefited from life in Egypt, Pharaoh's fearmongering policy works such that all of Egypt "came to dread the Israelites" (1:12). Horrifically, this leads Pharaoh to develop a policy whereby newborn male Israelites are put to death and thrown in the Nile (1:15–22). The tyrant option to leadership clearly operates through stoking fear of foreigners, imposing harsh slave labor on them, and then enacting violence.

The first-century Jewish philosopher Philo of Alexandria interprets the actions of Pharaoh as the grossest rejection of the practice of hospitality. The Israelites were strangers and refugees who were forced to flee Egypt for aid.[1] Philo emphasizes the vulnerable state of the Israelites as they present themselves as guests but find the Egyptians reducing them to prisoners of war: "In thus making slaves of men who were not only free but guests, suppliants, and settlers, the Pharaoh showed no shame or fear of the God of freedom and hospitality and of justice to guests and suppliants, who watches over such as these."[2] When God calls Moses to deliver the Israelites from the Egyptians, he tells Moses that he is a God who is of "a kindly nature and gracious to true suppliants" and will, therefore, punish those who violate hospitality laws.[3]

HOW NOT TO BE A TYRANT:
Hospitality to Strangers

Pharaoh exemplifies the way of Satan when it comes to dealing with strangers: He stereotypes, scapegoats, violently enslaves, and even kills. But there is an alternative practice that the Scriptures set forth for how God's people are to engage strangers. Central to both the Old and New Testaments is hospitality: using one's resources to make space for the stranger so that they can flourish and even become one's neighbor and friend.

WELCOMING THE STRANGER

Israel's experience under the tyrannical Pharaoh casts a long shadow on God's laws for how to treat strangers, sojourners, and immigrants. The Torah legislates a way of life for God's people that definitively rejects abuse and inhospitality toward the vulnerable—often offering a direct repudiation of Pharaoh's economic policy and treatment of immigrants.

In fact, the Christian Bible as a whole mandates that God's people be defined by hospitality to strangers. God blesses and rewards Abraham not only for his belief and obedience but also for his kind and hospitable welcome of the traveling (divine) visitors (Gen. 18:1–15). Alternatively, God destroys Sodom and Gomorrah for their violent and inhospitable treatment of strangers (19:1–29). God loves strangers and demands that they be protected and treated fairly, but God judges and destroys both societies and individuals—like Pharaoh—who oppress and violate the vulnerable stranger living in the land. God demands that Israel love and protect the vulnerable:

> You shall not wrong or oppress a resident alien, for you were aliens in the land of Egypt. (Exod. 22:21)

> You shall not oppress an alien; you know the heart of an alien, for you were aliens in the land of Egypt. (Exod. 23:9)

> When an alien resides with you in your land, you shall not oppress the alien. The alien who resides with you shall be

> to you as the citizen among you; you shall love the alien as yourself, for you were aliens in the land of Egypt: I am the LORD your God. (Lev. 19:33–34)

The contrast with Pharaoh's exploitative economy, which uses and enslaves foreigners to secure surplus for himself, could hardly be more obvious. In addition to the call to Israel to remember how they were treated by Pharaoh, Israel is also simply told that God loves the stranger. Just as God "executes justice for the orphan and the widow" and "loves the strangers, providing them food and clothing," Israel must "also love the stranger, for you were strangers in the land of Egypt" (Deut. 10:18–19). Israelites must treat foreigners among them as their neighbors by giving them fair legal verdicts (Deut. 1:16–17), paying fair wages for work (Deut. 24:14–15), intentionally leaving behind some of the produce in their fields (Deut. 24:19–22; Lev. 19:9–10; 23:22), and including the foreigners in Israel's feasts and rituals (Deut. 16:11–14; Lev. 16:29). Similarly, Israel is commanded to give a portion of their agricultural produce (or money received for payment) as an offering to the Lord, a percentage of which is to be shared with the materially and socially marginal: orphans, widows, immigrants, and the Levites (Deut. 14:22–29; 16:11).

The New Testament depicts Jesus as a hospitable king who indiscriminately extends God's welcome to all people. Jesus's kingdom is to be likewise marked by generous hospitality to all, including tax collectors (Luke 5:27–32; 19:1–10), women (7:36–50; 10:38–42), sinners (15:1–2), and even religious leaders who oppose him (7:39; 11:37–54; 14:1–6). Jesus's hospitality meals are marked by joy, inclusivity, and a sense of God's presence as outsiders are transformed into friends and family.

Paul, too, speaks of Christ as a stranger-loving ruler who, because he extends hospitality to all people, demands that his followers be marked by giving and receiving welcome from one another (Rom. 15:7–8; 1 Cor. 11:17–34). In Paul's letters, we see him exhorting a master to welcome a slave as even more than "a beloved brother" (Philem. 15–17); expending massive time and resources to procure reconciliation in his relationship with the church in Corinth because they are one another's joy, despite having caused each other pain (2 Cor. 2:2–4; 7:8–10; 10:9); and insisting that the church's common meal is a time for unity between those of different socioeconomic, ethnic, and cultural backgrounds (Rom. 14–15; 1 Cor. 11:17–34; Gal. 2:11–14). Paul draws on the practices of hospitality and peacemaking to teach his churches how to work toward a common life marked by justice and love that allows for new patterns and possibilities of friendship and social arrangements.

Christ's people should not only extend hospitality to like-minded disciples of Jesus but also look for opportunities to do good to everyone. Paul especially expects that his churches are capable of finding some common ground and shared pursuit of societal good (Gal. 6:10; Phil. 4:8). So to the church in Thessalonica, he commands love for one another "and for all" (1 Thess. 3:12). At the end of the letter, he expands this call, saying that none should repay "evil for evil, but always seek to do good to one another and to all" (5:15). In the midst of this hostility, Paul encourages the church to work quietly and to pay attention to their own affairs (4:11)—without hellfire and brimstone messages of God's judgment, mockery or ridicule of pagan worship, or justification for retaliating in response to evils they have experienced.

One way Paul's churches are to do good to all is through extending hospitality to their enemies rather than seeking retributive justice. Paul exhorts his readers in Romans 12–13 to pursue what is good, specifically with respect to outsiders (12:14–13:7). Four times in these verses, Paul exhorts his church to refrain from violence, retribution, or returning evil for evil toward their enemies (12:14, 17, 19, 21). Undoubtedly, Paul's exhortations, specifically in verse 14 ("Bless those who persecute you; bless and do not curse them") and verse 17 ("Do not repay anyone evil for evil"), flow from Jesus's call to refrain from retaliation in the Sermon on the Mount (Matt. 5:38–45; Luke 6:27–36). Paul's teachings are deeply indebted to Jesus's interpretation of Leviticus 19:18 as calling for love of neighbor and even of enemy. Paul exhorts the church to "live in harmony" (Rom. 12:16) and to "live peaceably with all" (v. 18). He advocates for nonviolent conflict resolution when he tells the church to feed their enemies if they're hungry or to give them something to drink if they're thirsty (v. 20). His claim that offering hospitality to one's enemies will "heap burning coals on their heads" (v. 20) likely means that the offer of hospitality will result in reconciliation and overcoming conflict. Paul's repeated exhortations to refrain from evil or revenge help eliminate any possibility that Paul is calling believers to punish their persecutors. Rather, Paul expects that extending hospitality to one's enemy will lead the wrongdoer to turn from their hostilities, thereby transforming them from a stranger or enemy into a friend. Hospitality is the *good* practice whereby one can overcome *evil*—retribution, violence, and conflict (v. 21).

Instead of subscribing to Pharaoh's brutal inhospitality to strangers and his fear and scapegoating of society's most vulnerable, disciples of Jesus recognize that their identity as the people of God is founded on God's welcome of them into his family, and so they commit themselves to rejecting all forms of xenophobia and instead extend welcome to strangers and outcasts. Followers of Jesus are called to carefully evaluate whether the rhetoric of public and political figures is life-affirming for all or whether such speech trades on propagating fear and using scapegoating techniques against others. Rather than passing on faulty stereotypes about immigrants, Christians can educate themselves about the causes of migration so that they can advocate and work for more just and equitable treatment for all those created in the image of God. Most importantly, Christians can welcome the stranger through engaging in meaningful relationships with immigrants and refugees and through supporting and volunteering with agencies that, out of Christian convictions, resettle refugees and provide compassionate care for immigrants.

REFLECTION QUESTIONS

1. Who are the strangers, the others, or the outsiders in your midst? Have you seen examples where such people have been treated with inhospitality or

where fearmongering techniques have been used to stereotype them as dangerous?

2. In what ways can leaders—whether politicians, teachers, professors, or business managers—use their power to practice hospitality to strangers?

3

EXALT YOURSELF OVER AND ABOVE THE PEOPLE

Solomon

He will take one-tenth of your flocks, and you shall be his slaves. And in that day you will cry out because of your king, whom you have chosen for yourselves; but the Lord will not answer you in that day.

—1 Samuel 8:17–18

Solomon, the son of David and Bathsheba, was the second king of the Davidic dynasty. He is remembered for his great wealth, his God-given wisdom in answer to his prayer, and his building of the temple in Jerusalem. But his rule was also marked by taking whatever he desired so that he was exalted above his people—in antithesis to God's laws laid out for the good king. He was consumed with a passion for taking gold, horses, and women. The remarkably large number of resources consumed by Solomon and the royal palace placed an incredible burden on the people.

It has been said, most famously by Plato, that only the good philosopher is suited to be king, but that the philosopher, of all people, will not want to be king. Why the paradox? The philosopher is the only one, Plato thinks, who will truly reject the opportunities that kingship provides for personal luxury, pleasure, and absolute rule over others. In fact, history is filled with stories of leaders who have fought with all their might to be in a leadership position precisely so that they could use their power for personal wealth, pleasure, and luxury. But whereas the way of the tyrant is personal exaltation at the expense of the people, good leaders use their power and influence to benefit the people, serve them, and even bear their burdens.

DEUTERONOMY'S LAW OF THE ("GOOD!") KING

One of the most important passages in the Torah is the "Law of the King" found in Deuteronomy 17:14–20. The text is notable for how it restricts Israel's king from acting like a typical monarch by emphasizing what the king cannot do. The good king must not be like those of "all the nations" around Israel (17:14), especially in terms of acquisitive greed and taking. In fact, four times the text says that the king must not "acquire"—he must not *acquire* many horses for himself; he must not send others to Egypt to *acquire* horses; he must not *acquire* many wives; and he must not *acquire* very large amounts of silver and gold (17:16–17). The verb "acquire" dominates the depiction of a king who will take people, wealth, and agricultural produce for his own luxury. The negative references to Egypt ("He must not . . . return the people to Egypt in order to acquire more horses, since the LORD has said to you, 'You must never return that way again,'" 17:16) indicate that Israel's king is to embody a way of ruling that is directly antithetical to the extractive and acquisitive regime of Pharaoh.

The Law of the King is also remarkable for its emphasis on the king's primary task as being an example of submission and obedience to God. The singular command given to Israel's monarch is that he should write out, read, and obey God's law: "When he has taken the throne of his kingdom, he shall have a copy of this law written for him in the presence of the Levitical priests. It shall remain with him and he shall read in it all the days of his life, so that he may learn to fear the LORD his God, diligently observing all the words of this law and these statutes" (Deut. 17:18–19). The king is no different from the people he rules in terms of his subservience to God and God's commands. As such, he must never exalt himself above the other members of the community (17:20). This king will be just like the ruler described in Psalm 72—a leader who rules with justice, vindicates the poor, has pity on the needy, and destroys those who oppress the weak, and whose rule results in prosperity for all people. But the actual history of God's people bears witness to the tragic fact that very few of Israel's rulers put Deuteronomy's Law of the King into practice.

Solomon's Exaltation of Himself Above the People

Upon entering the land, Israel explicitly asks Samuel for "a king to govern us, like other nations" (1 Sam. 8:4–5, 20). While Samuel is grieved by this, God tells him that Israel's desire for this type of king is ultimately a rejection of God and the way of life embodied in the law. This king will not be the king of Deuteronomy 17 who takes the lead in Torah obedience. Rather, Samuel speaks on God's behalf to make clear that "the ways of the king" (1 Sam. 8:9, 11) will entail personal exaltation as he taxes and conscripts for his own gain. Samuel prophesies that this king will *take* sons and daughters; *take* the best fields, vineyards, and olive orchards; *take* one-tenth of the grain; *take* male and female servants as well as young men and donkeys; and *take* one-tenth of the flocks (8:11–18). The king's building of an army will result in the conscription of young men as soldiers and older men as commanders. The king will force men to farm his land and care for his livestock. Women will be used in the king's palace and for domestic work. The Israelites will, in other words, be reduced once again to slaves. The similarities to Pharaoh's extractive and exploitative economy are obvious. And tragically, unlike the time of the exodus when Israel cried out for God's redemption from the oppression of Pharaoh (Exod. 2:23–25), now the people will "cry out" because of the oppression and abuse by their own king—but the Lord will not answer them (1 Sam. 8:18). The history of Israel's kings is marked by their use of power to take what they desire for their own benefit, with King Solomon providing the clearest example.

The rule of King Solomon is notoriously ambiguous. He asks God for wisdom and, on occasion, is described as walking in the ways of King David (e.g., 1 Kings 3:3–28). Sadly, he is also the perfect exemplar of a king like those of other nations who, through taxation and conscription, exalts himself over his people—with disastrous consequences.

In fact, he explicitly embodies the ways of Pharaoh. First, the echoes of Israel's enslavement are sounded in Solomon's conscription of 30,000 Israelite men for forced labor to build the temple (1 Kings 5:13). Solomon is portrayed as a skilled builder of cities, houses, and the temple, but all of this is accomplished through conscription and forced labor (9:15). The echoes of Pharaoh's economic policies are also evident in Solomon's use of non-Israelite slave labor (9:20–21) to build "storage cities" (9:19)—the same word used to describe Pharaoh's oppression of the Israelites in compelling them to build the "supply cities, Pithom and Rameses, for Pharaoh" (Exod. 1:11). In the royal court, Solomon finds twelve officials who are required to provide food for the king and his retinue one month out of the year (1 Kings 4:7). This heavy taxation provides the groundwork for anger and later revolt. Solomon requires an incredible amount of flour, oxen, cattle, sheep, deer, gazelles, roebucks, and fowl to feed the palace, and this exerts serious burdens of labor, time, and financial resources on those Solomon rules (4:22–23).

A disgusting example of a later king following in Solomon's footsteps is King Ahab (1 Kings 21:1–19). When Ahab sees a beautiful vineyard near his palace, he offers to pay Naboth, the owner, to acquire it. The problem standing in the king's way, however, is that this is Naboth's ancestral inheritance, and so Naboth refuses the king. Ahab's wife Jezebel, however, is more cunning, and she devises a plan to unjustly put Naboth to death so that Ahab can acquire the vineyard he so desires. Jezebel then says to Ahab, "Go, take possession of the vineyard of Naboth the Jezreelite, which he refused to give you for money" (1 Kings 21:15).

Returning to Solomon, he violates every aspect of Deuteronomy's Law of the King. He is marked by a great passion for the accumulation of gold (Deut. 17:17). Shields, thrones, drinking vessels—everything of Solomon's is made with gold. The narrator notes that nothing was made of silver, since silver "was not considered as anything in the days of Solomon" (1 Kings 10:21). Solomon is a devoted collector and trader of horses and chariots, also in violation of Deuteronomy 17:17 (see 1 Kings 10:26–29). With some level of irony, the narrator notes that Solomon acquires his horses from Egypt, again emphasizing the ambiguity of Solomon's kingship (1 Kings 10:28–29).

Finally, Solomon takes numerous foreign women as wives, thereby failing to heed the warning of Deuteronomy's Law of the Good King (Deut. 17:17). Solomon marries the daughter of Pharaoh (1 Kings 3:1). After Solomon's marriage to the daughter of Pharaoh, he takes wives from all the nations that God had commanded the Israelites to not marry from, lest the wives turn the Israelites to the worship of false gods (11:1–4).

The origins of the Davidic dynasty are sadly marked by powerful men seeing beautiful women, lustfully desiring them, and taking them at any cost. Solomon's father David is the most notorious example of a singularly powerful king who sees the beautiful woman Bathsheba while she is bathing and takes her for himself, despite her being married to Uriah (2 Sam. 11:1–5). When the prophet Nathan shares his parable of a wealthy shepherd who takes for himself the one beloved lamb of a poor man, he underscores David's wicked use of power by repeating the word "take"—"he took the poor man's lamb" (12:4); "you have taken his wife to be your wife" (12:9).

One of the next stories in 2 Samuel depicts how David's son Amnon follows in his father's footsteps, lustfully desiring Tamar and using both deception and violence to rape her before discarding her (13:1–19). While Solomon is not described as using violence to procure his wives, Solomon's clinging to his foreign wives in love is portrayed as leading him away from devotion to God (11:4).

How Not to Be a Tyrant: Bearing One Another's Burdens

The way of the tyrant is, as we have seen, to exalt oneself over and above the people one is tasked with leading. The tyrant takes what he desires, and the people give of their labor, wealth, resources, and even their very bodies to please the king. But the Christian Scriptures advocate a different way for the good leader, one that stems from the leader's love and devotion to God: bearing the burdens of the people.

Bearing One Another's Burdens

The primary task of Israel's kings is not to exalt themselves over their subjects but to take the lead in obedience to the Torah—and this results not only in worship of God but also in a way of life marked by justice and righteousness for the people. The wealthiest and most powerful king in Israel's history may be Solomon, but it is Josiah who is the paradigmatic good king and the one who most fully embodies the practice of loving God and his people (2 Kings 23:25). Josiah gathers together Israel's leaders to implement the peoples' devotion to God's teachings. He does not exalt himself above the people but rather obeys the law "with all his heart and all his soul" (23:2–3; cf. Deut. 6:5).

Israel's prophets look forward to a day when God's people will be ruled by a king like Josiah, who loves God and therefore cares for the needs of the people. There are many examples of such prophecies to choose from, but the most powerful is from the prophet Ezekiel. Ezekiel anticipates a time when God will judge those leaders who profit off the people:

> Thus says the Lord God: "Ah, you shepherds of Israel who have been feeding yourselves! Should not shepherds feed the sheep? You eat the fat, you clothe yourselves with the wool, you slaughter the fatlings; but you do not feed the sheep. You have not strengthened the weak, you have not healed the sick, you have not bound up the injured, you have not brought back the strayed, you have not sought the lost, but with force and harshness you have ruled them." (Ezek. 34:2–4)

The prophet delivers a blistering word from God against those leaders who use their position of leadership and power to exploit those they have been tasked with leading. God therefore promises a day when he will send a Good Shepherd who will accomplish God's task of caring for the people. This shepherd will search for the lost sheep and rescue them, heal them and bind their wounds, strengthen the weak and give food and drink to the hungry and thirsty, and judge all the wicked shepherd-rulers who have harmed the people (Ezek. 34:11–24).

Jesus, of course, is the singularly perfect good king who loves his people and bears their burdens. In fact, "the law of Christ" is nothing less than following the exhortation to "bear one another's burdens" (Gal. 6:2). The phrase "the law of Christ" echoes Paul's earlier claim in the letter that the Torah's fulfillment is found in "one word": "You shall love your neighbor as yourself" (Gal. 5:14; Lev. 19:18). Christ is the good king who embodies Leviticus 19:18, the one who loves his neighbor as himself (Gal. 2:20).

Paul consistently calls those with power and influence to lead in a way that is congruent with the law of Christ. He frequently asks those among his first-century audience with higher status or power to lower themselves and to use their influence and resources for the good of others. For example, husbands must sacrificially love and care for their wives (Eph. 5:25–28); wealthy homeowners must use their houses as a place to care for, rather than shame, the have-nots (1 Cor. 11:17–34); and those with high-status spiritual gifts should seek the edification of the entire community and not their personal glory (1 Cor. 14:1–40). Bearing one another's burdens requires that we reject pride, selfishness, and greed. The way of Christ consistently uses power, authority, and resources for the good of all rather than as an opportunity for self-exaltation.

REFLECTION QUESTIONS

1. Do you have any personal experiences with leaders who started out leading well and caring for those in their charge but who were later corrupted by the power, status, or wealth that they accrued from their position?
2. Do you have any personal experiences with a leader who embodies Ezekiel's vision of a shepherd-king who searches for the lost and cares for them, heals their wounds, strengthens the weak, and protects them from those who would harm them (Ezek. 34:11–24)?

4

Use (or Abuse) Religion to Legitimate Your Rule

Jeroboam

Then Jeroboam said to himself, "Now the kingdom may well revert to the house of David. If this people continues to go up to offer sacrifices in the house of the LORD at Jerusalem, the heart of this people will turn again to their master, King Rehoboam of Judah; they will kill me and return to King Rehoboam of Judah."

—1 Kings 12:26–27

Jeroboam was the first king of Israel after the northern kingdom rebelled against the house of David due to the burdensome taxation policies of Solomon's son Rehoboam. Jeroboam ruled over Israel from around 931 to 910 BCE. He is depicted in 1 Kings as a capable and hardworking administrator and politician. But he is also remembered for establishing an idolatrous state cult to consolidate and protect his kingship and his new kingdom.

A common strategy among tyrants is to use religion and a veneer of piety for their own political goals. Those in power or seeking power can further legitimate their rule by cleverly manipulating religion and sacred texts for their own ends. Potential presidents and political candidates can make a show of their religious devoutness to curry favor with voters. They can extend invitations to leaders of faith communities as a means of offering religious sanction for political and military actions. And religious leaders are often willingly enticed by invitations from those in power to bless imperial actions. This tyrant strategy is not only found in politics; it's prevalent in the church. Have you ever heard a sermon, a devotion, or a town hall report where the leader declares that what God is doing aligns exactly with their personal agenda?

Maybe they have even picked a biblical text to make it seem as if their actions and decisions have the full backing of God and the Bible, saying things like:

> God raised up Moses and Aaron to lead his people. God was forced to judge and destroy those who criticized and complained against God's chosen leaders. Let's not be like Korah, who rebelled against God's leaders and thereby fell under God's judgment! (Num. 16)

> God has shown us the way forward. So as we take this vote, let's make sure that none of us have the heart of a Judas who betrayed the work of God! (Luke 22:21–23)

Perhaps you have wondered why it is that what God is supposedly doing always perfectly aligns with the leader's personal agenda and desires.

Or maybe you've heard a politician invoke a biblical text in order to justify disturbing legislation or governmental decisions:

> Paul got it right when he said that Christians need to obey the government, since God has handpicked the leaders he wants!

Romans 13:1–7 is a particular favorite among leaders and politicians who want to use biblical authority to justify their decisions. Always omitted, of course, is the literary context of the passage, which demands that Christians practice love for their enemies, extend hospitality to one another and strangers, and pursue peace with all people (Rom. 12:9–21; 13:8–14).

Jeroboam exemplifies the disturbing strategy of leaders who willingly use religion and piety not to give true worship to God but to accomplish their own personal political goals.

Jeroboam's Subordination of Worship of God to His Political Goals

We have seen that one of the defining features of Solomon's kingship is his exaltation of himself over his fellow Israelites and his use of heavy taxation and conscription in order to acquire for himself gold, horses, food and drink, and numerous wives. Sadly, Solomon's son Rehoboam continues and even intensifies the heavy taxation policies among his people. Upon Solomon's death and Rehoboam's exaltation as king, Israel's assembly makes a request to Rehoboam: "Lighten the hard service of your father and his heavy yoke that he placed on us, and we will serve you" (1 Kings 12:4). But the king refuses to listen to the wise advice of the older men who encourage him to adopt a more lenient policy (12:6–8). Instead, Rehoboam takes the counsel of the younger men who tell him to treat the people with even heavier policies of taxation and labor: "Now, whereas my father laid on you a heavy yoke, I will add to your yoke. My father disciplined you with whips, but I will discipline you with scorpions" (12:11; cf. 12:14). The language of increasing an already heavy yoke works to depict Rehoboam as a Pharaoh figure who exploits the people with impossible burdens of forced labor. Like the wicked shepherd-rulers of Ezekiel 34, Rehoboam plunders, exploits, and profits off the people he rules.

This is the context for the rise of Jeroboam. Jeroboam is portrayed as a capable and hardworking servant of the king, and Solomon puts him in charge of the forced labor (1 Kings 11:28). Incredibly, Jeroboam receives a promise from God through the prophet Ahijah that God is going to give Jeroboam rule over the ten tribes of Israel. Just as God gave David a kingdom and dynasty, God will do so for Jeroboam (11:29–37). But God places a condition on Jeroboam that God's presence will be with him and establish his kingdom only if he will "walk in my ways, and do what is right in my sight by keeping my statutes and my commandments, as David my servant did" (11:38). We have already seen this language used to describe King Josiah, and it is a frequent refrain that 1 and 2 Kings uses to evaluate a king's behavior: Does the king walk in the ways of David by devoting himself to keeping and teaching God's law, as Deuteronomy's Law of the King mandates (Deut. 17:14–20)?

Just as Ahijah prophesied, the ten northern tribes split from the house of David and create their own kingdom with Jeroboam as the ruler (1 Kings 12:16–20). But the very first act of Jeroboam indicates that he will not trust God to establish his kingdom by worshiping God and devoting himself to the Torah. Jeroboam knows that the religious center of Israel, as mandated in the book of Deuteronomy, is in Jerusalem, where the kings of David reside. And he knows that if his kingdom continues to worship God in Jerusalem, this could have disastrous consequences for the survival of his kingship and his new kingdom.

So Jeroboam builds two rival sanctuaries, one at Dan in the north and another at Bethel in the south (1 Kings 12:28–30). Jeroboam is a creative and religious innovator, establishing sacred shrines, temples, altars, priests, and festivals to rival Jerusalem. He creates two calves of gold and declares to the people: "You have gone up to Jerusalem long enough. Here are your gods, O Israel, who brought you up out of the land of Egypt" (12:28). Jeroboam both establishes and runs the new religious centers himself. His motives are clear: He worries that his kingdom, which has rebelled against the house of David, might revert back to Rehoboam if they do not have their own temples, priests, and festivals. In other words, Jeroboam co-opts religion in order to serve his political agenda. And by using religion to establish and protect the northern kingdom, Jeroboam's state has become idolatrous.

The subordination of religion to politics and kingly rule is exemplified later in the hostile encounter between the prophet Amos and Amaziah, the priest of Bethel. Amaziah tells Amos to go and do his prophetic work elsewhere and to "never again prophesy at Bethel, for it is the king's sanctuary, and it is a temple of the kingdom" (Amos 7:13).

As Jeroboam is making perhaps the first sacrifice at his new religious shrine in Bethel, he has a hostile interaction with a prophet from Judah who tells him that God will raise up a new king, Josiah, from the house of David, who will destroy the kingdom of Israel and the sanctuary in Bethel (1 Kings 13:1–5). But Jeroboam will not relent, and he increases his support for his kingdom's new religious centers (13:33–34).

Josiah will restore proper worship of God, in part, by destroying worship and religion that has been co-opted by political interests (2 Kings 23:1–25). When "the book of the law" (22:8), likely the book of Deuteronomy, is discovered, Josiah does exactly what God has prescribed for good rulers. He reads it aloud to the people and commits to give wholehearted, sincere worship to God: "The king stood by the pillar and made a covenant before the Lord, to follow the Lord, keeping his commandments, his decrees, and his statutes, with all his heart and all his soul, to perform the words of this covenant that were written in this book. All the people joined in the covenant" (23:3).

First and Second Kings repeatedly speak of the sin of Jeroboam as the reason for the later destruction of the northern kingdom. Despite receiving the promise that God would establish Jeroboam's kingdom if he would walk in the ways of David, Jeroboam instead uses religion to establish and maintain his personal political rule. For this, Jeroboam is consistently held up as the evil antithesis of the good king, the opposite of a true worshiper of God who does what is good for the people. Most of Israel's kings are, in fact, described as walking in the sins of Jeroboam (1 Kings 15:30, 34; 16:19, 26, 31). And Jeroboam's sins will indeed elicit God's great judgment on the northern kingdom (1 Kings 14:16; 2 Kings 17:21; 23:15).

How Not to Be a Tyrant:
Sincere Worship

A temptation common to all people of faith is to use the things of the faith—the rituals, institutions, and practices—for ends other than the sincere worship of God. The trappings of worship become opportunities to advance one's personal goals, whether those be political aspirations (as in the case of Jeroboam and other politicians), advancement in status and respect, or the expectation of material blessings and safety. In contrast, the Scriptures advocate a life of wholehearted and sincere worship of God, warning that to do otherwise results in worship that is self-serving and manipulative.

Sincere Worship of God

Let's look at two warnings the Scriptures offer to protect us from using worship for self-serving ends. First, worship of God is by nature insincere if one claims to love God but fails to love one's neighbors. The prophets continually remind Israel that worshiping God while oppressing or harming their neighbors is false worship. One can make sacrifices in the temple and even engage in fasting and prayer, but God rejects this as insincere and fraudulent if one fails to share their bread with the hungry or clothe the naked (Isa. 58:1–7). God even says that he hates the peoples' sacrifices, their observance of feasts and festivals, and their prayers (1:10–15). God will accept their worship if they "learn to do good; seek justice, rescue the oppressed, defend the orphan, plead for the widow" (1:17). The prophet Jeremiah castigates the people for thinking that they are immune from God's judgment since they have the temple and offer sacrifices:

> Here you are, trusting in deceptive words to no avail. Will you steal, murder, commit adultery, swear falsely, make offerings to Baal, and go after other gods that you have not known, and then come and stand before me in this house, which is called by my name, and say, "We are safe!"—only to go on doing all these abominations? (Jer. 7:8–10)

The temple will not provide protection for the people should they continue to harm and "oppress the alien, the orphan, and the widow" (Jer. 7:6). For true worship of God requires love and justice for neighbor.

The worship God desires is articulated by King David in the Psalms. Psalms 15 and 24 are particularly poignant and beautiful commendations of true worshipers as those who "speak the truth from their heart" and "who honor those who fear the LORD; who stand by their oath even to their hurt" (Ps. 15:2, 4). In Psalm 24, King David asks, "Who shall ascend the hill of the LORD? And who shall stand in his holy place?" His response is succinct: "Those who have clean hands and pure hearts, who do not lift up their souls to what is false, and do not swear deceitfully" (Ps. 24:3–4).

A second warning against insincere worship is given by Jesus, who shows us his deep knowledge of the human condition and the temptation that is endemic to all who desire to worship God: to do what is right but for the wrong reasons. Jesus calls this hypocrisy—the outward appearance of the pursuit of God betrayed by an inward preoccupation and obsession with oneself (Matt. 6:1–18). The chief goal becomes not sincere worship of God but being seen by others as religious and pious.

Jesus warns that, like Jeroboam, humans are prone to deceiving themselves into thinking that God is an object that can be manipulated or controlled. Those who give alms to the poor, pray, and fast are indeed doing the right thing, but the desire that motivates their righteous actions is sometimes not sincere worship of God but rather the thirst for recognition, honor, or approval. This is why Jesus describes God as the one who sees the things that are done in secret (6:4). Since only God is worthy of worship and sees all and knows all, Jesus encourages his disciples to practice their good deeds in private (6:6). God values the sincere worship of the believer who approaches God in humble prayer and is genuinely concerned with the needs of others. In the middle of these warnings against hypocrisy, Jesus teaches his disciples how to pray (6:9–13). By coming to the Father in humility and seeking *his* name to be glorified, *his* kingdom to come, and *his* will to be done, disciples can seek the help they need to reject the deceptive pull of hypocrisy and to worship God in sincerity. The result, then, will be that one's good deeds function to give glory to God rather than to oneself (5:16).

REFLECTION QUESTIONS

1. It is right to seek God's guidance and direction, but how can we make sure that we—or our leaders—are not merely "using" God by manipulating others to further an ultimately personal, even selfish agenda?
2. What are some ways we can apply Jesus's exhortations to practice our righteousness in secret?

5

Harm Your Enemies

Herod the Great

When Herod saw that he had been tricked by the wise men, he was infuriated, and he sent and killed all the children in and around Bethlehem who were two years old or under, according to the time that he had learned from the wise men. Then was fulfilled what had been spoken through the prophet Jeremiah: "A voice was heard in Ramah, wailing and loud lamentation, Rachel weeping for her children; she refused to be consoled, because they are no more."

—Matthew 2:16–18

Herod the Great ruled from 37 to 4 BCE. His identity is socially diverse in that he was Idumean by ethnicity, Hellenistic in culture and monarchical rule, Jewish by religion, and a friend and ally to the Romans. He is remembered as a loyal client king of Rome, a capable political and military figure, and a builder of cities, temples, and fortresses. But he is also depicted as cruel, angry, impious, and unjust. He had multiple wives and often treated them with jealousy, violence, and cruelty. Most shocking was his murder of his second wife Mariamne and her family, who, Herod believed, were looking to overthrow his rule.

The tyrant approach to leadership coheres with conventional wisdom that says it is okay to harm our enemies. My enemies, the tyrant approach goes, are a roadblock to the accomplishment of my goals or, perhaps even worse, a threat to my safety and welfare. Harming one's enemies might come through repeated acts of exclusion, through gossip that destroys the person's reputation, or through preventing the person from access to friends and other social networks. On a larger scale, think of all the tyrannical regimes that have depended on secret police agents to imprison, deport, or even murder those deemed enemies of a leader or state. Or consider states that use special police forces to threaten and terrify protestors and peace activists. The violence inflicted on others is typically legitimated as necessary for the greater good, to safeguard the people or to establish law and order. Tyrants indiscriminately use violence, even torture, because they delight in their powerful spectacle of force against their enemies. We will see that Herod the Great exemplifies the tyrannical approach of harming one's enemies—but that the way of King Jesus does no harm to an enemy and instead pursues peacemaking through forgiveness and reconciliation.

HEROD'S VIOLENCE AGAINST HIS ENEMIES

Herod the Great was a remarkably skilled ruler, at least from certain vantage points. He knew how to ingratiate himself with the Romans, was able to exterminate problematic groups of rebel bandits in Galilee, and successfully defeated his rival, Antigonus, in order to secure his royal throne. Herod supported a variety of building projects and presented himself as a generous benefactor both to his subjects and to neighboring peoples. His rebuilding of the Jerusalem temple advertised his role as a pious ruler devoted to his Jewish subjects. Herod was effective and skilled in propagating a public image that enabled him to remain in power.

But Herod was happy to use any method whatsoever to both procure and secure his kingship. Even within his own family, Herod put to death his brother-in-law (Aristobulus) and his grandfather-in-law (John Hyrcanus II). Supposing that his wife Mariamne and her family were seditiously plotting against him, Herod killed her too, along with her two sons. Herod also put to death his own son Antipater, who Herod believed was plotting against him as well. This is the context for the supposed quip made by the Roman emperor Augustus: "It is better to be Herod's pig than his son." The Gospel of Matthew's story, then, of Herod's attempt to murder the child Jesus—who is born "King of the Jews"—is perfectly in line with Herod's character.

Jesus's messianic kingship is a threat to the counterfeit and corrupt tyrants who use their power for personal benefit even as it harms other people. In this instance, it is Herod the Great who is threatened by Jesus's birth. Matthew describes the story of Jesus and Herod as a contrast between two kings and two kingdoms. When King Herod hears of the birth of the child Jesus, the one who has been born "king of the Jews," Herod is afraid (Matt. 2:1–3).

He begins a search-and-destroy program out of fear that this new king will threaten his rule, gathering the scribes and teachers of Israel to inquire if the sacred texts indicate where the Messiah will be born (2:4). Remarkably, Herod believes that Israel's Scriptures will accurately predict and foretell the birth of the Messiah, and yet Herod wants to kill the promised Messiah so that he can maintain his rule. The scribes and priests answer Herod's question by quoting Israel's Scriptures: "In Bethlehem of Judea; for so it has been written by the prophet: 'And you, Bethlehem, in the land of Judah, are by no means least among the rulers of Judah; for from you shall come a ruler who is to shepherd my people Israel'" (Matt. 2:5–6; quoting from Mic. 5:2, 4; 2 Sam. 5:2). The irony is that, as the scribes and priests accurately predict Jesus's birthplace, their quotation of these Scriptures also previews Jesus's central task of being the merciful and compassionate shepherd-ruler over God's people.

The Messiah's task of shepherding God's flock recalls the prophetic promises that anticipate a time when God will raise up a faithful king from the house of David who will bring justice, peace, and mercy for God's harassed flock: "I will set up over them one shepherd, my servant David, and he shall feed them: he shall feed them and be their shepherd" (Ezek. 34:23). The Scriptures that the scribes and priests quote from reactivate a theme that occurs throughout Israel's prophets: God's promise to rule his people in peace and security and to give them protection from their enemies through a shepherd-king from the house of David (Jer. 23:1–6; Zech. 9:16; 10:2–3).

Returning now to King Herod, we can see that he plays the role of the tyrannical ruler or false shepherd who rules God's people for his personal benefit. Three times Herod is referred to as "king," but this king embodies all the worst stereotypical aspects of evil tyrants (Matt. 2:1, 3, 9). Emotionally unstable, he is disturbed and troubled as soon as he hears of Jesus's birth (2:3). He colludes with the religious aristocracy to determine Jesus's birth (2:4). He tries to deceive and trick the wise men by asking them to report the Messiah's whereabouts (2:7–8). Herod turns Jesus and his family into refugees as they are forced to find safety in Egypt (2:13–15). But most disturbing is the unbridled anger and grotesque violence Herod uses to murder children under the age of two near Bethlehem (2:16–21). Herod's kingship operates according to the principle of using any means necessary to maintain his rule, even if it involves destroying and killing others.

HOW NOT TO BE A TYRANT:
Peacemaking

History bears witness to the common belief that it is justifiable, indeed often good, to harm your enemies. In fact, a conventional definition of "justice" in antiquity is that "justice benefits friends and harms enemies."[1] Hesiod says it like this: "Call your friend to a feast; but leave your enemy alone. . . . Be friends with the friendly, and visit him who visits you. Give to one who gives, but do not give to one who does not give."[2] Jesus, too, attests to this common view when he says, "You have heard that it was said, 'You shall love your neighbor and hate your enemy'" (Matt. 5:43). This conventional approach to justice has resulted in untold violence and, as we will see, is emphatically not the way of Jesus, who calls his people to refrain from all manner of harm and instead to pray for and bless their enemies.

PEACEMAKING

Christians must decisively reject the belief that the ends justify the means. God's kingdom will not come through violence or coercion, because God's kingdom is a peaceable kingdom. God does not ask so-called Christian leaders or rulers to establish godly purposes through godless methods. Christ's people do not persecute their enemies or take vengeance on them. Christ's people, rather, have access to a surprising form of power that works through nonviolent peacemaking.

Jesus's primary proclamation in Matthew's Gospel is the kingdom of heaven (e.g., 4:17, 23; 5:3, 10, 19–20), which contrasts with the kingdoms of the earth. One kingdom operates according to peace and mercy, whereas the other uses violence, deception, and coercion. The Messiah's rule is radically different from human assumptions about the meaning and purpose of power, authority, and kingship. Unlike Herod, who seeks to maintain a position of rule over others, Jesus refuses to use power or violence to exalt himself, instead dispensing mercy and compassion to others. According to Matthew, the deeds of the Messiah (11:2) consist of healing those who are oppressed. Those who beg for mercy ("Have mercy on us, Son of David," 9:27) receive it from the Messiah. The people are "harassed and helpless, like sheep without a shepherd" (9:36), because their leaders have used power to benefit themselves. To such people, Jesus's actions are merciful, and his teaching also emphasizes mercy.

When Jesus rejects Satan's offer of a kingship predicated on using power in self-serving ways (Matt. 4:1–11), he demonstrates that his kingship will use power differently and that he will call his disciples to do likewise. Jesus's Sermon on the Mount, for example, calls his disciples to reject vengeance, retribution, and violence, and instead to embrace honesty and love for neighbors and enemies (5:21–48). Christ's power is revealed in love, suffering, and truth—not in brute force. In the Beatitudes, Jesus pronounces a blessing on peacemakers and promises that they will be called "children of God" (v. 9). They are God's children because God's character is one of peace, love, and mercy toward all, and this reality is embodied in the messianic Prince of Peace (Isa. 9:6–7; 11:6–9).

One of the practices of peacemaking that Jesus demands of all his followers is forgiveness and the refusal to harm those who have harmed us. Jesus's peace is embodied in actions that work to reject vengeance and retribution against one's enemies and to seek out reconciliation and an end to hostilities. This type of peacemaking is spelled out in Jesus's Sermon on the Mount. Disciples of Jesus reject not only murder but also the anger that would lead to murder (Matt. 5:21–26). Disciples of Jesus do not live by the principle of "an eye for an eye and a tooth for a tooth"; rather, they are to "resist an evildoer" through methods such as turning the other cheek (5:38–42). Disciples of Jesus must love their enemies and even pray for their persecutors, since God himself loves both the righteous and the wicked (5:43–48).

Paul too describes Christ as the good king who uses power in surprising ways to make peace and create a kingdom people. Christ conquered and killed the "hostility" between Jew and gentile not through the typical weapons of political warfare but through his death on the cross: "But now in Christ Jesus you who once were far off have been brought near by the blood of Christ" (Eph. 2:13). The Messiah is clearly a warrior king who defeats and destroys the social enmity: He "has broken down . . . the hostility between us"; he "has abolished" the decrees and commands that had divided; he reconciles both groups into "one body through the cross" and he "[puts] to death that hostility through [the cross]" (Eph. 2:14–16). The result of the Messiah's death is the creation of a unified, peaceful body politic. Paul speaks three times of the Messiah as an agent of peace: "He is our peace"; he "mak[es] peace"; he "came and proclaimed peace to you who were far off and peace to those who were near" (2:14, 15, 17). This peace is the eradication of social enmity between Jew and gentile and the creation of "one new humanity"—that is, a peaceful, unified, single body (2:14–16). Like Jesus, Paul demands that citizens of Christ's kingdom practice forgiveness and reconciliation: "Bear with one another and, if anyone has a complaint against another, forgive each other; just as the Lord has forgiven you, so you also must forgive" (Col. 3:13).

REFLECTION QUESTIONS

1. Not all tyrants go to the extremes of murder, as Herod the Great did, to inflict harm on their enemies. But there are plenty of other ways that tyrants act vengefully against those who challenge them and their leadership. Have you seen any examples of this on a global or personal scale?
2. Rejecting vengeance and pursuing peacemaking is difficult. What are some of the roadblocks or challenges that have risen in your own life (or your community's life) when you have sought to be a peacemaker?

6

Use Your Freedom to Pursue Pleasure

Herod Antipas

When [the daughter of Herodias] came in and danced, she pleased Herod and his guests; and the king said to the girl, "Ask me for whatever you wish, and I will give it." And he solemnly swore to her, "Whatever you ask me, I will give you, even half of my kingdom."

—Mark 6:22–23

After the death of Herod the Great, the Roman emperor Augustus decided not to appoint another king to replace Herod. Augustus instead divided Herod's kingdom among three of his sons: Archelaus, Philip, and Antipas. Herod Antipas received the title of tetrarch rather than king and ruled over Galilee from 4 BCE until 38 CE. In 39 CE, he was banished to France for his repeated attempts to procure the title of king for himself.

Plato makes the surprising but accurate claim that the tyrant is actually the least happy of all people.[1] The tyrant supposes that his complete freedom to pursue pleasure, luxury, and whatever strikes his fancy will result in happiness. But for Plato, the tyrant's inability to understand what is good and just means that his freedom is actually slavery to his baser desires and, sadly, to his ability to pursue what will only make him—and his subjects—unhappy. Through the way of King Jesus, however, leaders can use their power for the good of others and curb any desires to the contrary.

Herod's Lack of Self-Control

Herod Antipas, tetrarch over Galilee from 4 BCE to 38 CE, was not technically a king. In fact, he was perhaps most well known for his repeatedly unsuccessful attempts to procure the title for himself! That Mark goes out of his way to refer to Herod as "king"—repeating the title four times in a span of six verses (6:22, 25, 26, 27)—suggests irony, giving insight into the evil operation of the kings and kingdoms of this world.

It is Herod Antipas's devotion to pleasure and capricious use of power that cause him to be an unhappy and unstable ruler. Antipas throws a banquet party for the powerful in his kingdom. The great ones, the commanders, and the first ones of Galilee are all present (Mark 6:21). The banquet scene is intended to function as a place of luxurious pleasure for Antipas and his powerful friends, a time for eating, drinking, dancing, and perhaps gratifying sexual desires.

At the party, the young daughter of his wife Herodias dances and pleases Antipas and his guests. Antipas can't control his sexual passions, bordering on lunacy as he twice begs the girl to ask him for whatever she wants from him, even up to "half of my kingdom" (6:22, 23). When the girl asks, at the direction of her mother, that John the Baptist's head be brought to her on a serving platter, this makes Antipas "deeply grieved," because he actually likes listening to John and knows that John is a holy and righteous man (6:20, 26). But he makes good on his promise so as not to embarrass himself in front of his guests. I wonder if another version of Plato's striking claim that "the tyrant is the least happy of all" could be Mark's portrait of the banquet scene, ending with John's head being placed on a dinner plate by the executioner, then brought to the girl, and passed to the mother (6:28)—a scene of royal power and luxury turned truly grotesque.

Mark crafts his story of Herod Antipas in a way that intentionally recalls the story of another biblical king who is notorious for his lack of self-control and capricious use of power: the Persian king Ahasuerus in the book of Esther. This Persian king also gives many banquets for the elites in his palace, the first one lasting for 180 days (Esther 1:4). The king holds a banquet with all kinds of wines, ordering all "to do as each one desired," and the drinking happens "without restraint" (1:7–8). The king's pride and sexual desire are on display as he, "merry with wine," desires to parade Queen Vashti "in order to show the peoples and the officials her beauty" (1:10–11). When she modestly refuses, the "king was enraged, and his anger burned within him" (1:12).

The Persian king is also unrestrained in his use of women to satisfy his sexual desires, as he then gathers the most beautiful young virgins from his kingdom for his personal harem (2:1–4). Included among these women is Esther, who "pleased [the king] and won his favor" (2:9).

In the meantime, Haman, the villain of the story and the threat to the survival of the Jewish people, plots a way to destroy Esther's people (3:1–15). But Esther pleases the king so greatly that he asks her *three times* to make a request of the king, saying, "It shall be given you, even to half of my kingdom" (5:3, 6; 7:2)—the phrase Herod echoes in Mark. But whereas Herodias's daughter asks and receives the head of John the Baptist on a platter, the young Esther procures the salvation and protection of her people (Esther 7:1–8:17).

The protagonist of the story is clearly not the Persian king Ahasuerus. He is a classic tyrant who is devoted to luxury and pleasure, easily angered when manipulated and emotionally unstable and lacking control of his desires—remarkably like Herod Antipas. Yet the palace court of Herod, a Jewish king, is even worse than that of the Persian king, as Antipas is manipulated by his wife and daughter not into saving a righteous prophet but into accomplishing his grisly beheading.

Herod Antipas uses his power to pursue and successfully accomplish his desires. Yet Antipas is enslaved to his sexual passions. He makes wildly ridiculous oaths and promises. He engages in capricious and absurd acts of violence against the righteous. Tragically and ironically, Antipas does exactly what he does not want to do in putting

John the Baptist to death. If this is freedom to pursue one's desires, then it is remarkably self-defeating.

How Not to Be a Tyrant: Self-Control

The ancient and biblical virtue of self-control perhaps has connotations that are somewhat austere and even negative. Deep down many of us might agree with the sentiment rejected by Paul, "Let us eat and drink, for tomorrow we die" (1 Cor. 15:32). But in the story of Herod Antipas, we have seen what life looks like for someone with the power to pursue worldly pleasure but with no vision of what is good and just. It is a gruesome portrait of slavery to one's basest passions. The way of Jesus both uses power for the good of others, particularly the vulnerable, and actively restrains selfish desires that would neither make one truly happy nor result in good for others.

Self-Control

In the story that immediately follows Antipas's murder of John the Baptist, Mark shares another story that centers on a meal—the well-known story of Jesus feeding the crowd (6:30–44). This story gives a contrasting portrait of royal power as Jesus uses his power for the good of others rather than for personal self-gratification, pleasure, or fame.

The characters in the story are the "many" (rather than the great ones and first ones) who are pressing on Jesus. The setting is the wilderness rather than the royal palace. And even though Jesus is hungry, tired, and looking for a quiet place to rest, he has compassion on the great crowd "because they were like sheep without a shepherd" (Mark 6:34). Jesus teaches his disciples to use their gifts and power to serve others as he commands them to help him feed the crowd (6:37, 39). The multitude eats and is satisfied as they share in the messianic feast (6:42–44). In this passage, Mark is drawing on Numbers 27:16–17 in his portrait of Jesus as a Moses-like shepherd and leader of the people. And the episode resonates powerfully with Ezekiel 34, where the prophet anticipates a day when one will come from the house of David who will lead, nourish, feed, and save the lost sheep who have been scattered and exploited by Israel's corrupt leaders.

Using our power, authority, and influence for the good of others requires making war against any selfish, base desires that would harm another. The wisdom of self-control is exemplified in the teaching that King Lemuel receives from his mother in the book of Proverbs: "Do not give your strength to women, your ways to those who destroy kings. It is not for kings, O Lemuel, it is not for kings to drink wine, or for rulers to desire strong drink; or else they will drink and forget what has been decreed, and will pervert the rights of all the afflicted" (Prov. 31:3–5). The king's mother rightly connects a life of luxury and lack of self-control with injustice against the vulnerable.

Jesus not only reaffirms that his disciples should reject coveting, inscribed in the Torah as the tenth commandment, but also calls his disciples to reject the selfish internal desire of the heart that would long for what doesn't belong to them—in this instance, sexual pleasure from someone else's wife (Matt. 5:27–30). It's striking how many stories the Old Testament contains of men with power inflicting sexual harm on women. Shechem's rape of Dinah (Gen. 34:2), Judah and Tamar (Gen. 38:1–30), David's rape of Bathsheba and murder of Uriah (2 Sam. 11:1–27), and Amnon's rape of Tamar (2 Sam. 13:14) all point to the truth of God's words spoken to Cain: "Sin is lurking at the door; its desire is for you, but you must master it" (Gen. 4:7).

The tyrant longs for power so it can be used to gratify base personal desires, but King Jesus calls us to always use power for good and to eradicate desires that would harm others. This is why Paul speaks of self-control as a fruit of the Spirit (Gal. 5:23). Paul begins the list of the fruit of the Spirit with love and concludes with self-control precisely because self-control is a capstone to the list and demonstrates one's willingness to forgo personal desires that fail to embody love, sacrifice, and gentleness toward others. Christ's people, through the work of the Spirit, should engage in eradicating such evil desires to the point that Paul can speak of them as having "crucified the flesh with its passions and desires" (5:24).

REFLECTION QUESTIONS

1. Mark's Gospel juxtaposes the way of the tyrant Herod Antipas (6:17–29) with the way of Jesus (6:30–44). Does the contrast stimulate your imagination to make any contemporary comparisons between the pursuit of pleasure and luxury versus self-control?
2. How can the way of Jesus encourage us to work to prevent sexual harm against the vulnerable and/or to respond to concrete instances when powerful people sexually harm others?

7

Act as Though Truth Does Not Exist

Pontius Pilate

Jesus answered, "You say that I am a king. For this I was born, and for this I came into the world, to testify to the truth. Everyone who belongs to the truth listens to my voice." Pilate asked him, "What is truth?"

—John 18:37–38

Pontius Pilate, the Roman governor of Judea from 26 to 37 CE, went out of his way to antagonize, annoy, and even use violence against his Judean subjects. Described by Philo of Alexandria as being "naturally inflexible" and having "ceaseless and supremely grievous cruelty,"[1] Pilate offers a valuable lesson for aspiring tyrants: Whether you believe in truth or not, you must devote yourself to acting as though truth does not exist. Truth and falsehood are necessarily related to right and wrong, morality and immorality. So if truth doesn't exist, your subjects have no grounds for distinguishing between justice and injustice. They simply have no solid moral basis on which to criticize your decisions and how you wield your power.

Tyrants operate according to the principle of "might makes right." In fact, one of my favorite war stories, "The Melian Dialogue," found in Thucydides's account of the Peloponnesian War, exemplifies this maxim. In the story, Athens uses their superior military to coerce the island of Melos to their side in the war with Sparta. When the Melians appeal to morality and justice in an attempt to preserve their neutrality, the Athenians say that they have absolutely no interest in listening to claims about the gods, truth, or morality. Rather, they say the world works in such a way that "the strong do what they can, and the weak suffer what they must." In other words, might makes right. Power trumps truth.

The tyrannical regime is predicated on power and strength; justice, truth, and facts have nothing to do with it. The laws of rule are nothing less than power, force, and strength. The Athenians exemplify a characteristic of tyrants: manipulating truth, facts, and reality in order to serve the agenda of the powerful. And those who appeal to truth and justice are often derided by the tyrant as naive and ineffectual. Jesus, however, proclaims a kingdom of truth that is for the freedom and good of all people (John 8:32; 18:36–38). Jesus is, in fact, the embodiment of truth (14:6).

PILATE'S INDIFFERENCE TO TRUTH (AND JUSTICE)

When Jesus declares to Pilate, "You say that I am a king" (John 18:37), his statement brings the Gospel's theme of Jesus's kingship to a climax. Three times throughout the chapter, Jesus refers to his kingdom, one revealed not in political power but in his revelation of the Father to humanity. Jesus's kingship is centered on declaring the truth through his teachings and embodying that truth with his life—even to the point of death. What is the truth that Jesus has testified to? That God's kingdom is defined by

God's self-giving love for people (John 3:16–17; 10:11–18). That Jesus, as the one sent by the Father, has been entrusted with the power to pronounce a just sentence of life instead of death over his subjects (5:22–30). And that he himself, Jesus, is the very revelation of God (1:16–18; 14:6–7).

Pilate, standing in front of Jesus, is confronted with the claim that Jesus's kingdom of truth means that there is a real world. Reality—right and wrong, good and evil—does indeed exist. Truth is a given, not invented through coercion, powerful force, or deception. Might does not make right, since justice and injustice are real.

But Pilate, as a representative of imperial Rome, shows no interest in the truth and rejects any commitment to justice. Pilate knows that Jesus is innocent and is undeserving of death. Further, Pilate receives a personal invitation to respond to the truth of Jesus's kingdom, yet he responds, "What is truth?" (John 18:38). Pilate's question shows that he not only has no understanding of what truth is but that he also has no desire or commitment to act in accordance with that truth. The conversation is over. Face-to-face with the true king, Pilate responds with indifference, chaos, and fear.

Pilate first rejects the plea from the Jewish leaders to try Jesus, responding, "Take him yourselves and judge him according to your law" (John 18:31). Pilate knows that the

Jews want to put Jesus to death but do not have the legal power to do so, so his exhortation functions as a humiliating reminder that he is in charge, the only one capable of trying Jesus.

After his conversation with Jesus, Pilate declares, "I find no case against him" (John 18:38). Pilate shifts from exhibiting marked indifference to the case to acting as a master of chaos and spectacle. Given the Jewish custom (albeit nowhere else attested) to have a prisoner released on the Passover, why not, Pilate asks, release "the King of the Jews" (18:39)? Pilate's injustice is on full display. He knows that Jesus is innocent and that the case against him is without merit, but he uses Jesus to antagonize the Jewish leaders by declaring him to be their king—a claim they decisively reject (19:7). Pilate knows they want Jesus executed, but he toys with the leaders in offering to release him as a Passover gift. Pilate initiates the mock royal coronation of Jesus, which leads to the soldiers dressing him up in a purple robe, weaving a crown of thorns, giving obeisance to the supposed king with the acclamation "Hail! King of the Jews" (19:1–3). Pilate not only shames and tortures Jesus but also plays with and provokes the Jews by mocking Jesus as their king. Given an opportunity to pursue truth and justice, Pilate instead heightens the chaos, as the spectacle brings the Jewish people to the boiling point in their desire for Jesus's death. Twice more, Pilate says, "I find no case against him" (19:4, 6). Pilate knows Jesus is innocent but sets his crucifixion in motion anyway.

The irony is thick throughout the sham trial as Pilate judges Jesus from the bench of supposed justice (John 19:8–16). But who is ultimately on trial? Pilate's indifference to truth and his lack of commitment to justice provide a memorable depiction of a fraudulent ruler. The true judge is the one who willingly lays down his life for his people (10:11–18). Pilate's decision to write the *titulus* over Jesus as "Jesus of Nazareth, the King of the Jews" in Hebrew, Latin, and Greek reminds us of Jesus's promise to draw all people to the life-giving love of God through his death (11:48–52; 12:31–32). Jesus's kingship is one that Pilate could not, or would not, try to understand, since it is a kingship of truth—the truth that the crucified one is a king of justice and love.

How Not to Be a Tyrant: Tell the Truth

If there is no such thing as truth, or if truth and falsehood are impossible to determine, there are devastating consequences for morality and justice. Tyrants have a vested interest in using falsehood and deception to prop up their rule. One might say that their rule and their power depend on convincing others that truth does not exist or that truth is simply whatever the tyrant says it is. But the way of Jesus maintains that truth exists and that commitment to truth is necessary for living justly.

Truth-Telling

The way of Jesus entails utter commitment to believing in and telling the truth. Tyrants build and legitimate their rule through lies and deceit. Propaganda advertises that empires are eternal and invincible and that peace is established through violence. Tyrants, as we have seen, willingly receive honors that belong to God. Tyrants use their power to scapegoat and terrorize the weak and the vulnerable. As such, tyrants and empires have a vested interest in using their power to create a fictional world built on propaganda to convince their subjects that their rule is inevitable and that resisting their wickedness is futile.

The Scriptures frequently decry both leaders who propagate falsehoods and subjects who tolerate them (Ps. 12:1–5; Jer. 6:13–14; 7:4, 8–10). Amos condemns those who knowingly reject the truth for their own gain: "They hate the one who reproves in the gate, and they abhor the one who speaks the truth" (Amos 5:10). Similarly, Isaiah says: "Justice is turned back, and righteousness stands at a distance; for truth stumbles in the public square, and uprightness cannot enter. Truth is lacking, and whoever turns from evil is despoiled. The LORD saw it, and it displeased him that there was no justice" (Isa. 59:14–15). Israel's prophets repeatedly connect a willingness to avoid the truth and to propagate lies with injustice and violence—something clearly embodied in Pilate's treatment of Jesus.

Christ's people must instead testify with their words and lives to the truth that God alone is worthy of worship. Jesus himself testified before Pilate that the true ruler, the Good Shepherd, rules not by means of coercive force or rhetorical deception but through laying down his life for his people (John 10:11–18; 18:33–37). The truthfulness of King Jesus's claim is embodied in his taking his royal throne on the cross, the act that reveals God's love to draw all people to himself. In fact, Jesus's royal exaltation through the cross is the very act that reveals the rulers of this earth as fraudulent and counterfeit (12:31–32).

The book of Acts depicts the apostles as utterly devoted to the truth as they speak to the religious authorities "with all boldness" (2:29; 4:13, 29, 31). They claim that they will obey God rather than humans (4:19; 5:29) and use their voice to challenge and resist tyrannical power. In their willingness to speak truth to power, they demonstrate the integrity of their convictions and suffer as a result (4:21, 29; 5:28–33).

Revelation exposes both the counterfeit rule and the false pretensions of the emperor as it sets forth only the crucified king as "worthy" to receive divine honors (Rev. 5:1–6). The right response, then, is exclusive worship of the true king: "They sing a new song: 'You are worthy to take the scroll and to open its seals, for you were slaughtered and by your blood you ransomed for God saints from every tribe and language and people and nation; you have made them to be a kingdom and priests serving our God, and they will reign on earth'" (5:9–10). The primary vocation of God's people in Revelation is to offer worship and truthful testimony that Christ alone is the good and benevolent king (5:11–14; 7:10–12, 15–17; 11:15).

Christ's subjects are also tasked with actively sharing in his rule, not through military violence of any sort but through offering testimony to the truth. The Christian martyr Antipas (not to be confused with Herod Antipas) is Christ's "faithful witness" who testifies in refusing to offer worship to the emperor (Rev. 2:13, 20–24). Revelation exposes that standing behind the idolatrous claims of the emperor are the satanic powers of the dragon, the beast, and the false prophet (12:1–14:5). God's people conquer not through violence but through resisting idolatry and giving worship to God and the Lamb by being a people committed to testifying to the truth (12:11).

REFLECTION QUESTIONS

1. Have you witnessed instances of the tyrant approach to truth, such as the manipulation of truth, facts, and reality to serve the agenda of the person in power?
2. Do you know of any inspiring examples of Christians who have remained committed to speaking truth to power, even risking personal suffering in order to do so?

8

Believe That You Are Truly Great

Herod Agrippa I

You said in your heart, "I will ascend to heaven; I will raise my throne above the stars of God; I will sit on the mount of assembly on the heights of Zaphon; I will ascend to the tops of the clouds, I will make myself like the Most High."

—Isaiah 14:13–14

Herod Agrippa I ruled from 37 to 44 CE over his grandfather Herod the Great's regions and had the good favor of the Roman emperor Caligula, from whom he received the title of king. Agrippa received the lands that Herod Antipas ruled when Antipas was banished in 39 CE, and then in 41 CE he received Judea, Samaria, and Idumea from the emperor Claudius. He now reigned over all of Herod the Great's territories, but for only three years. Both Acts 12 and the Jewish historian Josephus narrate his sudden death.

Sophocles's tragedy *King Oedipus* tells the horrifying tale of how Oedipus disregards a prophecy that he would kill his father and marry his mother. If you aren't familiar with the story, I won't ruin it for you. Suffice it to say that the king's downfall stems from his refusal to listen to the advice of others and his determination to prove the legitimacy of his kingship. The story ends with the gouging out of his eyes and the death of his mother.

Stories of hubris—meaning excessive arrogance and overestimation of one's importance—are some of the most famous of all the ancient legends and myths. Achilles, Odysseus, Icarus, and numerous kings in the Greek tragedies exemplify both the personal longing for increased power and social status *and* the dangers of hubris.

Undoubtedly, there is something enjoyable in seeing a god or a king overestimate their abilities and then come to a tragic and often disturbing downfall. The stories also contain a moral lesson, a warning that individuals with power must be careful lest they destroy themselves and their families and communities.

Stories of hubris can be found in abundance today as well. Think of the CEO, the movie producer, or the megachurch pastor whose power and influence leads him to believe that his extramarital liaisons will go undiscovered. Or the pastor who expects his elders and church board to always carry out his wishes and protect him from criticism rather than provide wise counsel and godly advice. Or the university president who is obsessed with his presidential image and frequently advertises his personal accomplishments to get his way with the board of trustees. The way of the tyrant is one of hubris and almost invariably leads to a tragic downfall, but the way of King Jesus is the way of humility.

AGRIPPA'S HUBRIS

Herod Agrippa I is violent and angry, and he longs for public acclaim and honor above all. Acts gives us one reason for Agrippa's use of violence: his public acclaim and the popularity it wins for him. Like Pharaoh of the exodus generation who exterminated Hebrew boys at their birth (Exod. 1–2), like his grandfather Herod the Great who kills Jewish boys in Bethlehem (Matt. 2:16–18), and like his uncle Herod Antipas who beheads John the Baptist (Mark 6:14–29), Herod Agrippa I is a wicked tyrant who uses violence to achieve his goals. But the only goal for his persecution of the church in Jerusalem, his execution of James, and his imprisonment of Peter is to increase his popularity with his constituents—"After he saw that it pleased the Jews, he proceeded to arrest Peter also" (Acts 12:3).

Herod Agrippa is not just a violent man but also an angry tyrant. Acts doesn't provide the details, but we know that subjects were often dependent on their rulers for benefactions, specifically as it pertained to procuring grain and other sources of food. For whatever reason, Herod is angry with his constituents in the regions of Tyre and Sidon, and so the people must negotiate a peaceful resolution by working through the king's adviser. The people's ability to eat—their access to the food supply—depends on appeasing the anger of the king (Acts 12:20).

Against this backdrop, Herod appears before the people and prepares to deliver a public address. Acts tells us that he is clothed in royal attire (12:21). Kings and emperors often sought to impress the people through a beautiful and imposing appearance, and royal clothing played an important role in this. The Roman emperor Caligula, for example, is said to have tried to clothe himself with "the form of a God," even establishing a temple for himself and then dressing in the same clothes as the ones on his statue in the temple.[1]

The people are in a precarious position. Herod has demonstrated his use of violence against his enemies. Now, he is angry with the people, and their economy and food supply are dependent on the king's good graces. They therefore respond to the king's speech with perpetual shouting: "The voice of a god, and not of a mortal!" (Acts 12:22). The repeated acclamations are a means of offering worship and divine honors to Herod Agrippa.

Are the people simply engaging in flattery of the king? Perhaps. But in the ancient world, divine honors were often given to rulers who gave great benefits and gifts to their people. Caesar Augustus, formerly Octavian, wrote a public autobiography that advertised "the achievements and gifts of the god Augustus" for which in response "the senate passed decrees in praise of me."[2] In other words, divinity is, in this view, less a matter of essence and more a matter of supremely high status that stems from powerful gift-giving. If gods are those who exercise great power, then a king is godlike.

How Not to Be a Tyrant: Humility

Countless are the number of leaders—both political and within the church—who have used their position of power and influence to pursue worldly fame and greatness. But these so-called famous leaders come and go.

I am reminded of the well-known poem "Ozymandias" by Percy Bysshe Shelley, which speaks of a traveler who comes across a now broken and destroyed statue of the great King Ozymandias, a statue that once advertised to all who approached, "Look on my works, ye Mighty, and despair!" But the irony is contained in the next line: "Nothing beside remains." In other words, what is ultimately advertised by this once great king is that, despite his hubris, nothing much of his life or kingdom has lasted. Jesus calls disciples to turn from the futility of pride and hubris and instead to embrace the path of humility and self-forgetfulness.

Hubris vs. Humility

The Bible is not positive about this notion of divine honors and worship in exchange for powerful benefactions.

Instead, the Bible sees the willingness of rulers to accept and seek divine honors as pure hubris. The restored people of Israel are invited by Isaiah to mock and taunt "the king of Babylon" (Isa. 14:4), who boasts: "I will ascend to heaven; I will set my throne above the stars of God; I will sit on the mount of assembly on the heights of Zaphon; I will ascend to the tops of the clouds, I will make myself like the Most High" (14:13–14). Similarly, the prophet Ezekiel mocks the hubris of the king of Tyre, who tried to make himself like a god: "Your heart is proud and you have said, 'I am a god; I sit in the seat of the gods, in the heart of the seas,' yet you are but a mortal, and no god, though you compare your mind with the mind of a god" (Ezek. 28:2). Ezekiel anticipates a time of judgment and death for the prideful king that will demonstrate the futility and foolish hubris of his claims (28:6–10). Both Isaiah and Ezekiel contest and critique the claims made by these tyrants as acts of hubris, easily demonstrated by the fact that their thrones, kingdoms, and very lives are subject to mortality and God's judgment.

Perhaps the greatest critique of giving divine honors to humans comes from the apostle Paul's famous depiction of Christ in Philippians 2:6–11. Paul speaks of the Messiah as existing "in the form of God," meaning that he is truly deserving of "equality with God" (v. 6). Yet unlike the hubristic, self-deifying rulers, Christ does not exploit or take advantage of his divine status. Rather, by taking the form of a slave and submitting to death on the cross, the Messiah takes on public humiliation to rescue his people. True divine rule and power is seen, then, in the Messiah's refusal to exploit his equality with God. For this reason, God exalts him to a position of rule as Lord of the universe who alone deserves worship (vv. 9–11).

Those who belong to Christ are called to follow the same humble way of life. Specifically, Paul declares that the church must have the "mind" of Christ and must, therefore, live with one another in a manner that displays compassion, mercy, unity, and humility (Phil. 2:1–5). This requires practical wisdom whereby communities learn how to think, deliberate, and make decisions that flow from Christ's example of self-lowering. Paul's friends and colleagues, such as Timothy and Epaphroditus, embody a way of life that is centered on rejecting their own selfish interests and pursuing what is good for the broader community (2:19–30).

In another letter, Paul explicitly commands Christ's people to cultivate a way of thinking that rejects a foolish overestimation of one's importance: "By the grace given to me I say to everyone among you not to think of yourself more highly than you ought to think, but to think with sober judgment, each according to the measure of faith that God has assigned" (Rom. 12:3). Paul goes on to say that this way of thinking and making sober judgments about how to live should be exemplified in interpersonal relationships marked by generosity, hospitality, patience, and peacemaking (vv. 9–18). Rather than pursuing honor and greatness for oneself and at the expense of others, Paul makes the shocking exhortation to "outdo one another in showing honor" (v. 10).

Returning now to Herod Agrippa I, Acts tells us that God immediately strikes him down for his refusal to give glory to God as he receives divine honors from humans (Acts 12:23). God's way of being in the world, seen in the person of Jesus, is not one of grasping honor or demanding flattery. Christ's people, rather, follow the path of humility and worship God alone. Acts is clear that there is one God and that no human is worthy of worship or divine honors. There is a great gap between human kings and the humiliated and resurrected Messiah. He alone is Lord of all (10:36).

REFLECTION QUESTIONS

1. Why are humans, especially leaders with some level of influence and charisma, so often prone to believing that they are uniquely great?
2. Given that Jesus reveals divine power through lowering himself to rescue humanity, do you think there are certain popular misunderstandings of humility?

9

GIVE GIFTS AND FAVORS TO THE ELITES

Caesar Augustus

But [Jesus] said to them, "The kings of the Gentiles lord it over them; and those in authority over them are called benefactors. But not so with you; rather, the greatest among you must become like the youngest, and the leader like one who serves. For who is greater, the one who is at the table or the one who serves? Is it not the one at the table? But I am among you as one who serves."

—Luke 22:25–27

Caesar Augustus, the adopted nephew of Julius Caesar, ruled over Rome from 27 BCE until 14 CE. He brought an end to the Roman civil war and presented his reign as the beginning of an era of peace and prosperity. Augustus was a master propagandist who depicted himself as divinely elected to inaugurate a golden age for Rome. Virgil's *Aeneid* (6.791–96) foretells this coming "son of a god" whose reign will be marked by peace, piety, virtue, and agricultural prosperity for all.

The first century BCE of the Roman Republic was defined by civil war. Powerful military men like Marius, Sulla, Pompey, and Julius Caesar used their own armies to fight one another for control of Rome. Octavian, later renamed Augustus, brought the war to an end in his defeat of Mark Antony at the Battle of Actium in 31 BCE. Upon avenging his uncle Julius Caesar against his assassins, Augustus declared that he was returning the Republic back to the senate and the Roman people.

His legacy is quite complicated. While he made a show of not acting as a monarch and frequently declared that he accepted no honor that wasn't in accordance with Roman customs, he was undeniably the ruler of Rome and the inhabited world, and everyone knew it.

He accepted titles such as "Father of the Fatherland," "Pontifex Maximus," and, of course, "Augustus Caesar." Given that his adoptive uncle Julius Caesar was deified, Augustus also was known as the "son of a god." Augustus willingly propagated the belief that he had ushered in a golden age.[1]

AUGUSTUS'S STRINGS-ATTACHED GIFT-GIVING

One of the primary ways that Augustus, among other Roman emperors, perpetuated his rule was through public benefactions and gifts, which took the form of building projects, like public baths and theaters, and the provision of games and entertainment, money, and food. But these were never considered to be free, for it was understood that the recipient was now indebted to the giver. In exchange, Augustus received public displays of gratitude and honor, such as honorific inscriptions, good seats at public events, wreaths, and statues. Perhaps most significantly, Augustus's benefactions commanded absolute loyalty and gratitude from his subjects.

Augustus wrote an autobiography called the *Res Gestae* (translated as "the things done"), which he set up in public places as an advertisement of his deeds, many of which were his gifts to the Roman people. The text begins:

> Translated and inscribed below are the achievements and gifts of the god Augustus, which he left engraved at Rome upon two bronze tablets. When I was nineteen years old, I got ready on my own initiative and at my own expense the army by means of which I set the state free from the slavery imposed by the conspirators. On account of these things the senate passed decrees in praise of me and enrolled me into the senate in the consulship of Gaius Pansa and Aulus Hirtius, giving me the status of an ex-consul in offering advice and it gave me rods of office. It entrusted to me as *Propraetor* together with the consuls the task of taking precautions that nothing should harm the state. In the same year, when both consuls had fallen in war, the people appointed me consul and chose me for the office of triumvir in charge of the settled order of the state.[2]

The text reads as one long list of benefactions he granted to the empire, demonstrating his unparalleled honor and worthiness to rule. A few examples will suffice.

> Peace: "It is agreed that the gate of War, which our ancestors desired to be closed once all land and sea was at peace under the Romans, has before me, since the foundation of the city, in the whole era been closed twice only, whereas

> under my leadership the senate voted for it to be closed three times."
>
> Money: "Four times I supported the treasury with my money, until I paid out 37,500,000."
>
> Buildings: "I built the senate house and next to it the *chalcidicon*, and the temple of Apollo on the Palatine with its porticoes, the temple of the god Iulius, the shrine of Pan."
>
> Games: "Three times I gave gladiatorial shows in my name and five times in the names of my sons or grandsons. . . . Twice I presented to the people in my name the spectacle of a contest of athletes summoned from every side and for a third time in the name of my grandson."[3]

Augustus's benefactions also included paying for his own army to secure peace from civil war, protection from foreign threats, basic amenities of grain and oil, cash for male citizens and army veterans, and hosting games and festivals. These benefactions are one of the primary ways that Augustus maintained relationships with other elites. Not only did he provide food, buildings, and games for his subjects but he also gave land grants, senatorial offices, tax relief, and money for expenditures to other elites whom he deemed worthy. Those elites who wished to make economic and political advances needed the emperor's benefactions to do so. And their receipt of his gifts further established them in loyalty, gratitude, and devotion to Augustus.

But whom did Augustus's gifts really benefit? The answer is that these benefactions were primarily oriented toward elevating other elites to solidify and maintain Augustus's own rule. Augustus's favors and gifts did not have as their goal the benefit of the impoverished and lowest stratum of society—the poor, the old, the ill, and the orphaned. The gifts were not even given for the sake of benefiting any so-called middle class. Participating in Augustus's system presumed that you had something valuable to offer in return—in other words, something that only other elites had access to.

How Not to Be a Tyrant: Prophetic Critique

In the first installment of *The Godfather*, Don Vito Corleone (played by Marlon Brando) is asked for a large favor from another father, Bonasera, attending the don's wedding.

Vito grants the favor and responds, "Someday, and that day may never come, I will call upon you to do a service for me." The man may indeed receive the gift he's asked for, but strings are attached to the gift and his life is now ultimately in service to the godfather's will and agenda. When Don Corleone comes to ask for a favor, Bonasera will have no choice but to reciprocate. The way of Jesus rejects all forms of exploitative economics and gift-giving, knowing that this provides an unfair advantage for those without access to these gifts and creates situations of bondage to those who receive the gifts.

PROPHETIC CRITIQUE OF EXPLOITATIVE ECONOMIES

In the epigraph above, Jesus declares that Roman rulers wield power and authority through benefactions in a tyrannical way to increase their power and to lord their authority over their subjects. The official narrative that the Roman emperor offers is that he pursues the good of his subjects through giving benefactions. But Jesus says these kings lower themselves not to serve but rather to use their power for their own benefit (Mark 10:41–45; Luke 22:24–27).

Jesus's claim that greatness is instead found in sacrificial service, embodied in his table fellowship and service, is a radical inversion of how Augustus used his benefactions to receive honors and to benefit other elites. Jesus repeatedly teaches and exemplifies the truth that his economy is an inversion of the world's values. For in the kingdom of God, it is the child who is the greatest (Matt. 18:1–5). Mercy is to be given to the homeless, the imprisoned, and the poor—those who have nothing to give in return (25:31–46). The way of King Jesus is one where acts of mercy, compassion, and hospitality—especially for the vulnerable, poor, and marginalized—are granted without any expectation for human reward. This way of life is the antithesis of the way of the tyrant exemplified by Augustus.

Augustus used material and public depictions to advertise his powerful rule and its legitimacy. Among many examples is the *Gemma Augustea*, a large carving that depicts Augustus seated next to the goddess Roma and crowned by another deity, who gifts him with rule over the entire world. The message is clear: Augustus is the earthly representative of the gods. He has their political, military, and economic backing. In fact, Augustus is depicted as bringing peace and harmony to Rome and the known world through violent subjugation of his enemies.

In contrast, the book of Revelation is harsh toward the imperial economics of benefaction, arguing that the system uses exploitative practices to benefit the elites.

Revelation exposes the goddess Roma as a prostitute who adorns herself with luxury, symbolically referring to Rome as "Babylon the great" (Rev. 17:1–2, 5; 18:7). The Roman emperor exploits his people so that the elites might have access to "gold, silver, jewels and pearls, fine linen, purple, silk and scarlet, all kinds of scented wood, all articles of ivory, all articles of costly wood, bronze, iron, and marble, cinnamon, spice, incense, myrrh, frankincense, wine, olive oil, choice flour and wheat, cattle and sheep, horses and chariots, slaves—and human lives" (18:12–13). Rome is so addicted to consumption and luxury that it even trades in human lives for its benefit. While it is hard to have exact statistical certainty, many have proposed that 25–30 percent of the population in Roman Italy were slaves.[4] The slave trade—made possible through trafficking captured humans through warfare—provided Rome with a source of free labor to benefit the wealthy and elite.

Augustus's peace is marked by slavery, military violence, and economic exploitation. The Roman emperor is no true benefactor who gives good gifts to the people; rather, he uses violence to exploit people for his own interests and for those of wealthy merchants and political officials. And because of this, Revelation describes a time when God will destroy the pretensions of Rome for its extravagant luxury and consumptive greed (Rev. 18:3, 7, 9, 11–14); for its economic system that benefited imperial elites at the expense of the majority (vv. 15–19); for its exploitative practices of slavery and trading human lives (v. 13); for worshiping wealth, luxury, and consumption (v. 7); and for persecuting the righteous and those who criticize Rome's economic, political, and military idolatry (vv. 20–24). Roma's boast, spoken in the guise of the ancient Babylon the Great, "I rule as a queen; I am no widow, and I will never see grief" (v. 7), gives voice to the economy's idolatrous self-divinization and belief that luxury, consumption, and acquisition—even at the expense of the good of others—will fulfill one's deepest desires.

Surprisingly, Jesus exhorts his people to "give to everyone who begs from you" (Luke 6:30). Self-interested gift-giving, hoping that giving a gift will put someone in your debt or will increase your social standing, is not allowed. In the Acts of the Apostles, we even see Barnabas selling off his land—land that could have been used to advance his social status and to become a so-called benefactor—so that his resources can be used for those in need (Acts 4:32–37). Jesus's call to share one's gifts without discrimination flows from his understanding that God is a merciful and generous gift-giver to both the righteous and the unrighteous (Luke 6:32–36). The way of Jesus calls for people to be openhanded, as Jesus was, with mercy and gifts to those without great status, power, and wealth.

REFLECTION QUESTIONS

1. Do you think the current economic arrangements of your society unfairly benefit the privileged few?
2. Revelation presents a scathing prophetic critique of the Roman economy's willingness to exploit humans for the sake of the wealthy's consumptive greed and love of luxury goods. John even hears a voice exhorting him to refrain from sharing in the sins of this economy (Rev. 18:4). What would it mean in our contemporary context to seek to refrain from economic injustice?

10

Use Terror to Control Religious Minorities

Nero Claudius Caesar

And I saw a beast rising out of the sea, having ten horns and seven heads; and on its horns were ten diadems, and on its heads were blasphemous names. . . . Also it was allowed to make war on the saints and to conquer them.

—Revelation 13:1, 7

Nero ruled as the Roman emperor from 54 to 68 CE. His early reign was considered to be something of a golden age after the more turbulent and abusive rules of Caligula (37–41 CE) and Claudius (41–54 CE). Nero was popular with both the propertied classes and the ordinary people, even if his passion for his own singing and playing of the lyre was deemed excessive by many. Nero's cruelty was also notorious. He ordered his mother Agrippina to be drowned and, when that failed, stabbed, as a result of her opposition to his affair with Poppaea Sabina. He forced the philosopher Seneca to commit suicide. And when Rome suffered a devastating fire, he blamed the Christians and burned many of them alive.

When tyrants face crises or challenges to their leadership, one way to deflect attention from themselves is to find a group of people, often a religious or ethnic minority, and place the blame on them. But the way of Jesus calls his people to be a hospitable presence who seek the welfare and common good of all people.

Nero's Reign of Terror

The earliest followers of Jesus were a strange and, to some, a potentially dangerous and seditious religious cult, because the primary prerequisite for joining the Christian community was rejecting ancestral gods and ceasing to give worship to them. Paul reminds the Thessalonian church of how the surrounding regions have heard that the church had "turned to God from idols, to serve a living and true God" (1 Thess. 1:9). For followers of Jesus in Paul's time, there was only one true and living God. The rest of the so-called deities were either idols or demons, and Christians were not to be involved in any way with temples, sacrifices, and prayers to these false gods (1 Cor. 10:19–21). Paul even refers to the worship of these gods as "worthless" as he calls his audience to worship the living God (Acts 14:15).

To most outsiders, then, Christianity was entirely bizarre and potentially a dangerous superstition. The ancient world simply assumed that people would worship their ancestral deities. Failure to do so was tantamount to rejecting one's history, family, and civic obligations. The worship of one's ancestral gods was also seen as an essential civic duty, since a city's flourishing was dependent on it. So to cease making sacrifices to the gods was to risk their wrath in the form of famine, earthquake, or war. When Peter reminds his readers that Christ's death ransomed them from "futile ways inherited from your ancestors" (1 Pet. 1:18), he makes the ethnic and social consequences of their conversion to Christ clear: Conversion requires the repudiation of their religious history and ancestral traditions. For Peter's readers, the tensions were likely exacerbated by some pagan wives and slaves converting to Christianity, thereby seemingly subverting the order of the patriarchal household (2:13–3:7).

Christians also refused to worship the Roman emperor. The second-century church father Tertullian notes that Christians "are public enemies—because they will not give the Emperors vain, false and rash honours."[1] Tertullian testifies to widespread blame of Christians for any and every crisis and disaster: "If the Tiber reaches the walls, if the Nile does not rise to the fields, if the sky doesn't move or the earth does, if there is famine, if there is plague, the cry is at once: 'The Christians to the lion!'"[2]

Most Christians not only refused to worship the emperor but also refrained from participating in Roman social life, such as visiting the baths or partaking in the spectacles of gladiatorial games and theater. Many early Christians also abstained from joining the military or holding political office. Their withdrawal from public activities made them an easy target to blame. Christians were perceived as religious minorities, a superstitious cult that threatened the well-being of the empire, and were treated with suspicion, if not outright slander and violence. First Peter repeatedly speaks of non-Christians hurling verbal abuse at their Christian neighbors, maligning them as "evildoers" (2:12), reviling them "for the name of Christ" (4:14; also 2:15; 3:9).

Christians provided the perfect scapegoat for the fire in Rome in 64 CE. Of the fourteen districts in Rome, ten were seriously damaged. While Suetonius, among others, claims that Nero himself was responsible for starting the fire, Tacitus reports that Nero blamed the Christians for the fire and heinously tortured them. Nero's scapegoating tactics also commenced a period where Roman governors and magistrates, as well as local officials even outside of Rome, accused Christians of wicked and wild rumors of incest and cannibalism. As a result, some Christians were put on trial for advocating seditious customs. Both Suetonius and Tacitus report that it was during Nero's reign that Christians were referred to as having a superstitious religion.[3] Both in Philippi and in Thessalonica, Paul was accused of advocating anti-Roman customs and of proclaiming that Jesus was a rival to the emperor (Acts 16:20–21; 17:6–7).

The book of Revelation depicts Nero (and possibly later Roman imperial rulers as well) by using the symbol of a violent beast that makes false and pretentious claims to divinity (Rev. 13:1, 5–6). The beast demands that all people give him worship, and so the multitudes make blasphemous claims: "Who is like the beast, and who can fight against it?" (13:4). The beast is a personification of Roman political and military power. Even after the beast receives a mortal head wound—likely an allusion to Nero, who used a sword to commit suicide—the wound is healed and the beast recovers (13:3–4; 17:7–8). Roman imperial power persists. And it uses its powers to make violent war against the saints (13:7).

Revelation testifies that the Christian refusal to worship Rome's gods and the Roman emperor resulted in violent death for some. The risen Christ speaks to the church in Pergamum: "I know where you are living, where Satan's throne is. Yet you are holding fast to my name, and you did not deny your faith in me even in the days of Antipas my witness, my faithful one, who was killed among you, where Satan lives" (Rev. 2:13). There are martyrs who have "been slaughtered for the word of God and for the testimony they had given," who cry out for God to avenge their deaths (6:9–11). And the goddess Roma will fall and be judged, not least for her collaboration with the beast in violent persecution of "the witnesses to Jesus" (17:3, 6; see also 11:7; 17:14; 18:24). Rome's so-called peace depends on violence—not only the violence of subjugating, conquering, enslaving, and taxing other nations but also a violence that is perpetrated against those who refuse to worship the Roman emperor and gods. Rome's peace is predicated on crucifixion and other forms of coercive terror and torture.

How Not to Be a Tyrant: Doing Good to All

Tyrants often welcome the terror, torture, and exclusion of minority populations because they view minorities as either a threat to their vision of a monolithic society or a convenient scapegoat to distract others from their own failures. But the way of Jesus does not call forth a people who seek power in order to coercively impose their vision of the good life on the world. In total allegiance to the one true God, followers of Jesus are instead to faithfully commit to seek the common good of all people.

Doing Good to All

Whereas the way of the tyrant employs terror to achieve its goals, the way of King Jesus calls people to pursue peacemaking in a violent world by doing good to everyone.

Followers of King Jesus will use their voice for resistance and prophetic critique of evil. But they are also called to do good to rulers, leaders, and a society that may be antagonistic to the way of King Jesus. The Scriptures are clear that God will hold kings, rulers, governors, and local officials accountable for how they wield their power. They are not supposed to be a terror for those who do good (Rom. 13:4). Governors serve their role when they "punish those who do wrong" and "praise those who do right" (1 Pet. 2:14). Respect and honor—not worship—are to be granted to the emperor (1 Pet. 2:17; Rom. 13:1–2). Good rulers should be pleased to have subjects who will offer prayers not *to them* but rather *on their behalf*, and they should allow Christians to live "quiet and peaceable" lives (1 Tim. 2:1–2).

While the tyrant willingly uses terror and abuse of religious minorities to achieve his goal, Christ calls us to entrust our cause to God and to seek the good and welfare even of those who would harm us. The experience of the people of God as a minority in the Diaspora is instructive for how followers of Jesus are to live. God's people are to reject the path of rebellion and revolt and are to instead "seek the welfare of the city" and "build houses and live in them; plant gardens and eat what they produce" (Jer. 29:5–7). Likewise, Daniel and his friends refuse to engage in any false worship of idols or foreign gods, and yet they also use their wisdom and skills to benefit King Nebuchadnezzar of Babylon (Dan. 1–6).

Peter repeatedly counsels Christians living as "exiles of the Dispersion" (1 Pet. 1:1)—almost certainly a symbolic designation of their status as religious minorities in Asia Minor—to embrace the strategy of "doing good" to all people. They are to honor, respect, and submit to those in authority (2:13–14). While they must give worship to God alone, they are exhorted to "honor the emperor" (2:17). Even if slandered, Christ's people are to repay evil and abuse with blessing and prayer (3:9). It is absolutely unacceptable, however, for anyone who bears the name of Christ to suffer as an evildoer: "But let none of you suffer as a murderer, a thief, a criminal, or even as a mischief maker" (4:15). Repeatedly, Peter reminds God's people that God alone has ultimate authority. "Therefore," Peter says to his readers and to us, "let those suffering in accordance with God's will entrust themselves to a faithful Creator, while continuing to do good" (4:19).

REFLECTION QUESTIONS

1. Is the ancient practice of scapegoating religious minorities still seen in the world today? If so, how should followers of Jesus respond if Christians are

the ones being scapegoated? How about if those of another religion or cultural group are the ones experiencing persecution?

2. Do you think the Scriptures' call to refrain from revolt and rebellion and "to seek the welfare of the city" (Jer. 29:7) can coexist with the practice of peaceful protest? Why or why not?

Epilogue

> Then I heard a loud voice in heaven, proclaiming, "Now have come the salvation and the power and the kingdom of our God and the authority of his Messiah, for the accuser of our comrades has been thrown down, who accuses them day and night before our God. But they have conquered him by the blood of the Lamb and by the word of their testimony, for they did not cling to life even in the face of death."
>
> —Revelation 12:10–11

What more can I say? For time would fail me to speak of Abimelech, Saul, Manasseh, Jezebel, Xerxes, Alexander the Great, Antiochus Epiphanes IV, and Caligula. The Scriptures carry out an ongoing antagonism between God's kingdom and plan for his people to work together for a good, peaceful, shared common life and those who use power in ways that ultimately reflect the values of Satan.

As you've read through the short vignettes of the Bible's tyrants, you may have recalled examples of tyrannical activity in those professing to follow Jesus. Perhaps, if you're like me, you've even wrestled with your own temptation to follow the more conventional and self-serving tactics and strategies of these rulers. Following Jesus requires a constant willingness to listen and commit ourselves to his teachings. My hope is that those of us who confess Jesus as Lord will renew our commitment to reject the way of the tyrant and to embody the alternative practices Jesus has taught us. In the meantime, I want to conclude with one final practice that marks the way of Jesus: the practice of hope.

Christ's people believe and confess that he is the singularly good and righteous ruler, even as they long for the full consummation of his kingdom when he returns. In the meantime, Jesus's disciples hope to worship God in peace as they pray for kings and leaders and reject outright antagonism or rebellion (Rom. 13:1–7; 1 Tim. 2:1–2; 1 Pet. 2:13–17). But Christ's people are capable of endurance in the midst of sufferings and tribulations and even under poor rulers because they know that one day Christ will be revealed as the true and rightful king of the world (Phil. 2:10–11; Rev. 17:14; 19:16). On this day, Christ will vindicate all those who were harmed, abused, and exploited by the powerful (Rev. 6:9–11). And Christ's people will actively participate in a restored, renewed world no longer marked by corruption and evil (Rom. 8:18–25; Heb. 2:5–10; Rev. 21–22).

Christ's people see the imperfections and even wickedness of current regimes, yet they trust the scriptural promise that God will one day fully rule the world through a righteous, just, and peace-loving king. This empowers them to entrust their lives and causes to God rather than to violent, coercive methods and to even put their bodies on the line in their resistance of evil and willingness to prophetically speak truth to power. Forgiveness, peacemaking, hospitality, and solidarity with the poor and the vulnerable may have the appearance of weakness, but they are right and good for people who have hope that God's purposes will come to a climax in the reign of Christ—the truly good king.

NOTES

CHAPTER 2 STOKE FEAR OF OTHERS

1. Philo, *Life of Moses* 1.34.

2. Philo, *Life of Moses* 1.36, in *Philo*, vol. 6, trans. F. H. Colson, Loeb Classical Library 289 (Harvard University Press, 1935), 295 (slightly modified).

3. Philo, *Life of Moses* 1.72–73 (LCL, 315).

CHAPTER 5 HARM YOUR ENEMIES

1. Plato, *Republic* 334, in *Plato's Republic*, vol. 1, *Books 1–5*, trans. Paul Shorey, Loeb Classical Library 237 (Harvard University Press, 1930), 31.

2. Hesiod, *Works and Days* 342, 352, in *The Homeric Hymns and Homerica*, trans. H. G. Evelyn-White, Loeb Classical Library 57 (Macmillan, 1914).

CHAPTER 6 USE YOUR FREEDOM TO PURSUE PLEASURE

1. Plato, *Republic* 9.577–89.

CHAPTER 7 ACT AS THOUGH TRUTH DOES NOT EXIST

1. Philo of Alexandria, *Embassy to Gaius* 301–2, in *Philo*, vol. 10, *The Embassy to Gaius*, trans. F. H. Colson, Loeb Classical Library 379 (Harvard University Press, 1962), 151, 153.

CHAPTER 8 BELIEVE THAT YOU ARE TRULY GREAT

1. Philo, *Embassy to Gaius*, in Philo, *The Embassy to Gaius*, trans. F. H. Colson, Loeb Classical Library 379 (Harvard University Press, 1962); Suetonius, *Caligula* 52.

2. Augustus, *Res Gestae*, heading and 1.2, in Allison E. Cooley, *Res Gestae Divi Augusti: Text, Translation, and Commentary* (Cambridge University Press, 2009), 59.

CHAPTER 9 GIVE GIFTS AND FAVORS TO THE ELITES

1. Virgil, *Aeneid* 6.791–94.

2. Augustus, *Res Gestae* 1.1–4, in Allison E. Cooley, *Res Gestae Divi Augusti: Text, Translation, and Commentary* (Cambridge University Press, 2009), 59.

3. Augustus, *Res Gestae* 13.1 (73), 17.1 (77), 19.1 (79), 22.1 (85).

4. Keith Hopkins, *Conquerors and Slaves: Sociological Studies in Roman History* (Cambridge University Press, 1978).

CHAPTER 10 USE TERROR TO CONTROL RELIGIOUS MINORITIES

1. Tertullian, *Apology* 35.1, in *Tertullian, Minucius Felix*, trans. T. R. Glover, Loeb Classical Library 250 (Harvard University Press, 1931), 159.

2. Tertullian, *Apology* 40.2 (183).

3. Suetonius, *Nero* 16.2; Tacitus, *Annals* 15.44.

JOSHUA W. JIPP (PhD, Emory University) is associate professor of New Testament at the University of Notre Dame. He is the author of several books, including *Reading the Gospels as Christian Scripture*, *Pauline Theology as a Way of Life*, *Saved by Faith and Hospitality*, and *The Messianic Theology of the New Testament*. Jipp also serves as coeditor for the Baker Exegetical Commentary on the New Testament. He lives in Chicago, Illinois.

CONNECT WITH JOSHUA

joshua.jipp

@jjipp101